10 LIES
MEN
BELIEVE

10 LIES

MEN
BELIEVE

J. LEE GRADY

Charisma
HOUSE
A STRANG COMPANY

Most STRANG COMMUNICATIONS BOOK GROUP products are available at special quantity discounts for bulk purchase for sales promotions, premiums, fund-raising, and educational needs. For details, write Strang Communications Book Group, 600 Rinehart Road, Lake Mary, Florida 32746, or telephone (407) 333-0600.

10 LIES MEN BELIEVE by J. Lee Grady
Published by Charisma House
A Strang Company
600 Rinehart Road
Lake Mary, Florida 32746
www.strangbookgroup.com

Unless otherwise noted, all Scripture quotations are from the New American Standard Bible. Copyright © 1960, 1962, 1963, 1968, 1971, 1972, 1973, 1975, 1977, 1995 by The Lockman Foundation. Used by permission. (www.Lockman.org)

Scripture quotations marked CEV are from the Contemporary English Version, copyright © 1995 by the American Bible Society. Used by permission.

Scripture quotations marked KJV are from the King James Version of the Bible.

Scripture quotations marked NIV are from the Holy Bible, New International Version of the Bible. Copyright © 1973, 1978, 1984, International Bible Society. Used by permission.

Scripture quotations marked NLT are from the Holy Bible, New Living Translation, copyright © 1996, 2004. Used by permission of Tyndale House Publishers, Inc., Wheaton, IL 60189. All rights reserved.

Scripture quotations marked THE MESSAGE are from *The Message: The Bible in Contemporary English*, copyright © 1993, 1994, 1995, 1996, 2000, 2001, 2002. Used by permission of NavPress Publishing Group.

Cover design by Nathan Morgan
Design Director: Bill Johnson

Visit the author's website at http://themordecaiproject.org/.

Library of Congress Cataloging-in-Publication Data:

Grady, J. Lee.
  10 lies men believe : the truth about God, women, sex, money, power, and real manhood / by J. Lee Grady. -- 1st ed.
        p. cm.
  Includes bibliographical references (p.   ).
  ISBN 978-1-61638-137-0
  1. Men (Christian theology) 2. Christian men--Conduct of life. I. Title. II. Title: Ten lies men believe.
  BT703.5.G73 2011
  248.8'42--dc22

                                        2010042547

E-book ISBN: 978-1-61638-402-9

First Edition

11 12 13 14 15 — 9 8 7 6 5 4 3 2 1
Printed in the United States of America

DEDICATION

To my dad, Jackson Lee Grady, who loved me unconditionally, provided for me generously, and modeled Christ in the way he treated my mother in more than sixty years of marriage.

To my sons-in-law, Rick and Sven: I am honored to call you my sons.

And to the men from other countries I have been able to encourage in recent years: Abraham, Adeyemi, Adolfo, Agus, Aleksandr, Alex, Arthur, Balint, Daniel, Enrique, Felipe, Femi, Fernando, Gabe, Gennady, Gideon, Iftakhar, Jackson, Javier, Jesús, Jusan, Kelechi, Kumar, Ladi, Luis, Marian, Marlon, Medad, Miracle, Mikhail, Moses, Nebby, Norberto, Oto, Peter, Raja, Ralph, Robert, Sabin, Shibu, Shyju, Sunil, Swanky, Tamas, Victor, Xavier, and Yinka. You are all humble warriors who inspire me.

CONTENTS

10 LIES

FOREWORD

by Napoleon Kaufman

FORMER RUNNING BACK FOR THE OAKLAND RAIDERS
PASTOR, THE WELL CHRISTIAN COMMUNITY
DUBLIN, CALIFORNIA

IT'S BEEN A long time since I've read a book that exposes sin within a culture and at the same time heals the culture. Lee Grady is to be commended for taking the bold step of writing *10 Lies Men Believe.*

In churches all over the world the Lord is trying to raise up a generation without compromise—a generation that is consecrated, faithful, and walking in the fear of the Lord. But we have a problem:

The church doesn't understand that in order to raise up strong spiritual sons and daughters, we need both the male and female genders. Because of tradition, bad doctrine, and in some cases religious spirits, the church has been handcuffed to the idea that women can't preach, prophesy, and lead within local churches.

These are lies that both men and women in the church have believed. But I believe that Lee, through this book, has taken this discussion a step further by addressing the practical everyday thought patterns that men deal with on a domestic level.

He lists many of the lies that men believe: "God made men superior to women." "Real men don't cry." "A man should never admit his weakness." These are lies that men inside and outside the church have bought into. These are lies that are so ingrained in the culture of this world that men have been affected by them regardless of their race, creed, or color.

Lee dispels these lies with the truth of God's Word and a heart full of grace and humility. This book is a must-read for men—especially those leading local churches. I say this because every day we as leaders are dealing with men who walk through the church doors looking for answers. Some have never had a father. Others have never been taught how to treat a lady. And many others have never had close male relationships.

We often teach men how to pray, fast, and prophesy, but we must also teach them how to be men! Being a man isn't about dominating your wife. We don't prove our manhood simply by having a job and bringing home money. Jesus demonstrated His manhood by laying down His life for His bride.

The message of Christ is totally countercultural, but it's what real men do. Lee Grady once again has captured the heart of God and has written a book that will challenge the religious spirit in our churches as well as the spirit of this age.

10 LIES

HAVE YOU BEEN BRAINWASHED?

WHAT MAKES YOU a man? If you've ever wrestled with that question, this book is for you.

Our dysfunctional culture sends mixed signals about manhood. The world of sports tells me that authentic masculinity is linked to athleticism, physical strength, and winning the game. In short, *muscles make the man.*

The world of finance suggests that my worth is directly tied to the size of my bank account, the square-footage of my house, the brand of watch I wear, and the make and model of car I drive. In other words, *money makes the man.*

Then Hollywood tells me that real manhood is measured by how long I can last in bed and how many women I've had sex with. The clear message is: *a penis makes a man.*

To add to that chorus, popular music today tells young urban men that their masculine value is boosted if they act tough, beat up women, use profanity, abuse drugs, outsmart the police, and drink as much alcohol as possible. If they do all these things, someone on the street will reward them by saying, "You da man!" So these guys grow up thinking that *bad behavior makes a man,* especially if it involves

1

impregnating as many women as possible—and leaving those women with black eyes, bruises, and broken hearts in the process.

Sorry to disappoint you, guys, but if that's the official criteria for manhood, then I don't win the badge. By the world's standards, I'm not qualified to write a book about the masculine journey.

First of all, I'm not a star athlete, and my lack of ability on the ball field was a painful issue for me during my childhood and teen years. I grew up in Alabama and Georgia, where football is a religion and star quarterbacks are its idols, at least on Friday nights and Saturday afternoons before everyone cleans up for church. I did not measure up to the godlike status of these gridiron titans. I could never figure out how to throw a perfect touchdown pass, nor could I block a guy whose forearms were thicker than my thighs. I wasn't even that good in sixth grade kickball—although I did learn to throw a mean Frisbee in high school.

Second, if money makes a man, again I fail the test. My first car, which my father helped me buy when I was in eleventh grade, was a Plymouth Valiant that had a hole in the floorboard. I graduated to a Honda Civic. When my wife and I started having children, we bought a used Dodge Caravan that often required repairs to the air conditioner. My salary gradually increased over the years, but because we had four children who grew up and went to college, I stayed in the low-budget category and bought a Hyundai Elantra that cost just slightly more than my oldest daughter's wedding.

I had some friends who started successful companies or got rich from selling real estate before the Great Recession. One friend of mine is an entrepreneur who sometimes has conference calls with billionaires. Some of these men have boats and summer homes, and they take vacations to Maui. Me? I live in the same two-thousand-square-foot, two-bath home that I bought in 1993, and I'm still paying for it. I don't own a Rolex, I don't have a stockbroker, and there is no gate at the entrance of my neighborhood. I'm just your average, middle-class Joe.

Third, if real manhood is determined by number of sexual partners, then I am a loser. True, I experimented with some heavy petting when I was in high school (in the front seat of my Plymouth Valiant), but I was too afraid of God's wrath and my girlfriend's father to cross the forbidden line. So I was a technical virgin when I got married, and so was my wife. We spent our entire honeymoon in Miami Beach figuring out how everything worked! (And I remind young men today that this is what honeymoons are for—to provide ample time for hands-on sex education.)

So I've made an honest confession. In the past I have felt extremely insecure about my own manhood. Yet when I examine these worldly concepts of masculinity, I realize that many men would actually be jealous of what I have.

On the physical side, so what if I can't bench press 250 pounds or win a Heisman Trophy? At least my wife thinks I'm sexy. Isn't that enough? (For the record, she doesn't think guys with huge pecs and biceps are attractive.) I try to jog three times a week, and I enjoy staying physically fit. But I don't have to compete with Mr. Universe. Why should I waste my energy comparing myself to every jock out there?

Financially, I really don't care if my savings account is smaller than Bill Gates's or Warren Buffett's. I know too many "successful" businessmen who lost their marriages and their children's respect on their way to the top. *Fortune 500* will never write about my salary or my stock options. Yet I don't have anything to complain about. I put my children through college without going into debt, I paid for my children's weddings (and their cars), and I support Christian ministries all over the world. I actually feel very blessed—especially when I realize that the majority of people in the world live on less than $1.50 a day.

When it comes to sex, I have what very few men have. My wife has faithfully loved me for twenty-six years. We've stayed true to our wedding vows, and our intimacy is just as satisfying today as it was when I was a more easily excitable twenty-five. My boring, one-woman lifestyle may not be of interest to the editors of *GQ* or *Playboy*, but studies prove that monogamous guys sleep more soundly and don't need prescription drugs to calm their feelings of guilt, anxiety, and fear of sexually transmitted diseases.

So if we are honest, we must admit that muscles, money, and multiple sex partners don't qualify us for true manhood. The world's standards are cheap and flimsy. The measure of a real man goes much deeper.

Let's Talk About It

1. What do you think makes a real man?
2. In what areas of your life—such as sports, money, professional success, or sex—have you struggled with insecurity about your manhood?

REAL MEN KNOW GOD

Just before I went to college back in the 1970s, I came face-to-face with the reality that Jesus Christ is God's Son and that He gave His life as a sacrifice for me. Even though I couldn't see proof of His existence, I knew in my heart He was real and that everything the Bible says about Him is true. So I chose to believe. I took a step of faith and gave Him ownership of my life, my future, and all my choices.

A true miracle happened to me in that moment. Christians call this experience *conversion*. Jesus actually told His friend Nicodemus that when we put our trust in Him and believe that He has the power to forgive our sins, we are "born again" (John 3:3). We receive a new nature because the very presence of Christ comes to dwell inside us. Our identity changes at the very core.

The apostle Paul described conversion this way:

Therefore if anyone is in Christ, he is a new creature; the old things passed away; behold, new things have come.

—2 CORINTHIANS 5:17

Paul also wrote:

I have been crucified with Christ; and it is no longer I who live, but Christ lives in me; and the life which I now live in the flesh I live by faith in the Son of God, who loved me and gave Himself up for me.

—GALATIANS 2:20

This is actually the secret of discovering your true identity as a man. It is the only path to authentic masculinity. If God made you a man, then it is only God who can give you total fulfillment in that identity. He holds the key to unlocking your manhood potential.

Many men think being a Christian is a sign of weakness. They think a "real man" depends on nobody but himself. But the truth is that the self-made man is a tragic figure. He may have some moments of pleasure and personal accomplishment, and he might accumulate some wealth, but at the end of his life he steps into a dark eternity with nothing.

You will never discover who you are by making more money, having more explosive sex, driving a nicer car, drinking the best beer, winning the most trophies, or getting your name in lights. Those things are just man's vain attempt to find significance. But when life ends, everything temporal fades away, including sex, money, cars, houses, beer, trophies, diplomas, and fame.

The journey to real manhood begins when we trade in our old nature—our past mistakes, shameful failures, pride, insecurities, fears, and the lies we have believed—and then allow Jesus to live through us. We need a personal relationship with Him. The Bible, more than anything, is a collection of stories about people who had encounters with God. They discovered His mercy and forgiveness; then, as they developed a personal relationship with God, He used them to do extraordinary things that changed the course of history.

This is the essence of Christianity. It is not a religion of strict rules or of gritting our teeth to avoid sin. True faith in Christ is about trading our weaknesses and inability for His amazing inward strength, which the Bible calls *grace*. He offers it to anyone who will simply believe in the Son of God. (If you have never put your faith in Jesus before, you can learn how to do that at the end of this introductory chapter.)

If you are already a Christian, that doesn't mean there won't be any bumps along the road to true manhood. If you are like me, you battle every day. Most of us men are insecure, and we bring our insecurities with us on this journey of faith. You probably also fight lust, anger, resentment, jealousy, and selfishness. You may be haunted by painful memories. We come to Jesus in a broken condition, and His healing process (which the Bible calls *sanctification*) takes time.

I wrote this book to help you navigate that journey.

While only the grace of God can change us, we also must submit to His work in us. A doctor only performs surgery on a patient who is lying still; we too must lie still on the Great Physician's table if we want true healing. That simply means we must be willing to submit our lives to His knife when cutting is necessary.

Part of that process is what the Bible calls *the renewing of the mind*. Romans 12:2 says:

> And do not be conformed to this world, but be transformed by the renewing of your mind, so that you may prove what the will of God is, that which is good and acceptable and perfect.

This is the ultimate in brainwashing. God uses the truth of His Word to wash our brains and flush out all the wrong ideas and worldly principles we have learned, whether from our families, friends, educational systems, or the media (as well as churches or other religious institutions that may have distorted the Bible).

We must confront the lies! And the only way to do this is with God's eternal principles, which are revealed in the Bible. The apostle Paul says that God's Word is like a sword (Eph. 6:17), and he said he was not afraid to use this spiritual weapon against wrong philosophies. We need the same courage.

Paul wrote in 2 Corinthians 10:3–5:

> For though we walk in the flesh, we do not war according to the flesh, for the weapons of our warfare are not of the flesh, but divinely powerful for the destruction of fortresses. We are destroying speculations and every lofty thing raised up against the knowledge of God, and we are taking every thought captive to the obedience of Christ.

All of us are bombarded today by the lies of culture. They come at us like poisoned arrows, flying from a dozen different directions. Many of these seductive lies are aimed at men in particular. They whisper to us:

- Everybody sleeps around today—even Christians! It's OK to shack up with your girlfriend. Besides, you need to find out if you are sexually compatible with her before you ask her to marry you.
- Pornography is everywhere, so you might as well indulge. Besides, your wife will never know.
- One quick affair with that young girl at your office won't hurt anyone.
- Everyone is dishonest at times, so go ahead and lie to your boss.
- Even though you don't have the budget to buy that sports car, go ahead and splurge. It will make you look good.

- You were justified in hitting your wife. She needs to learn a lesson and stop being so disrespectful!
- Psychologists say there's nothing wrong with homosexual behavior. Maybe you should experiment with it.
- You don't need close friends. The best way to get ahead is to watch your back and distrust everyone around you.

You have a choice. You can listen to this deadly onslaught of lies day after day until they sink in deep enough and eat you from the inside. Or you can pick up your spiritual weapons and fight. There really is no middle ground. If you want to be a real man, you must go on the offensive and engage the enemy.

In this book I am exposing ten of the most common lies that bombard men today. As you read, I invite you to pick up the sword of the Holy Spirit. Don't be a wimp. Dare to fight back. Take every thought captive, resist the devil's temptations, and become a true warrior.

Let's Pray About It

Father, I want to be a man of God. I don't want to be conformed to this world. Renew my mind according to Your Word. Break the power of any lies I have believed. Help me break free from any wrong mind-sets about what it means to be a true man. I surrender my life to You in every area so that Christ can live His life through me. Amen.

FIRST THINGS FIRST

Perhaps you realize that you have never surrendered your life to the Lord. Don't delay that decision! I encourage you to embrace God's amazing love today and receive the salvation that only Jesus Christ gives. Here are five simple steps you can take to begin a relationship with God:

1. **Recognize your need.** The Bible tells us that "all have sinned and fall short of the glory of God" (Rom. 3:23). All of us are sinners, and we must admit our need for a Savior.

2. **Repent of your sins.** Because God is completely holy and we are sinners, our sins create a wall that separates us from God. By confessing your sins and turning from them, you will find forgiveness. *Repent* means to make a 180-degree turnaround. The Bible promises, "If we confess our sins, He is faithful and righteous to forgive us our sins and to cleanse us from all unrighteousness" (1 John 1:9).

3. **Believe in Jesus.** This is the most important step! God worked a miracle when He sent His only Son to die so that He could pay for all our sins. Put your faith in Him and believe in His power to save you. The Bible says, "For God so loved the world, that He gave His only begotten Son, that whoever believes in Him should not perish, but have eternal life" (John 3:16).

4. **Receive His salvation.** God has given us this free gift, but we still must accept it. Thank Him for sending Jesus to die on the cross for you. Thank Him for His amazing love, mercy, and forgiveness. Then ask Him to live in your heart. His promise to us is clear: "But as many as received Him, to them He gave the right to become children of God" (John 1:12).

5. **Confess your faith.** The Bible assures us, "If you confess with your mouth Jesus as Lord, and believe in your heart that God raised Him from the dead, you will be saved"

(Rom. 10:9). You have been born again and are now part of God's family. Tell someone else what Jesus has done in your life!

If you have walked through these five steps, you can say this prayer:

Lord Jesus, thank You for dying on the cross for me. I recognize that You are the true Son of God, sent to Earth to pay the full price for all of our sins. I believe that You were raised from the dead and that You live forever in heaven. You are God Almighty, and I surrender to Your lordship. I am sorry that I have lived my life apart from You. Please forgive me for thinking that my life could have true meaning without You, My Creator and Lord.

I turn from my sins and choose to follow You. Please wash me clean and come into my heart. I give You all my hurts, my fears, my unforgiveness, my pride, my greed, and all the garbage of my past. Thank You that I can start my life over again with You. Amen.

Let's Talk About It

1. Describe briefly when and how you made the decision to put your faith in Jesus Christ.
2. We all come to Christ in a broken condition. What were some of the deepest struggles you faced when you first became a Christian?
3. What ongoing struggles do you face today?
4. Our culture tells us many lies about what makes a real man. Which ones are you most tempted to believe?

The relationship between the male and the female is by nature such that the male is higher, the female lower, that the male rules and the female is ruled.[1]

—ARISTOTLE, IN *POLITICA*

One hundred women are not worth a single testicle.[2]

—CONFUCIUS

It is only males who are created directly by the gods and are given souls. Those who live rightly return to the stars, but those who are "cowards" or [lead unrighteous lives] may with reason be supposed to have changed into the nature of women in the second generation.[3]

—PLATO, IN *TIMAEUS*

Men are the maintainers of women because Allah has made some of them to excel others and because they spend out of their property; the good women are therefore obedient, guarding the unseen as Allah has guarded; and (as to) those on whose part you fear desertion, admonish them, and leave them alone in the sleeping-places and beat them; then if they obey you, do not seek a way against them; surely Allah is High, Great.[4]

—THE QURAN, 4:34

Blessed art thou, O Lord our God, King of the universe, who hast not made me a woman.[5]

—ANCIENT PRAYER OF JEWISH RABBIS

The souls of women are so small, that some believe they've none at all.[6]

—SAMUEL BUTLER, ENGLISH POET

---

10 LIES

Lie #1

GOD MADE MEN SUPERIOR TO WOMEN.

MILLIONS OF WOMEN around the world are subjected to the horror of male domination. They are gang-raped in Latin America, their genitals are mutilated in parts of Africa, they are forced to wear burkas in Afghanistan, they are sold as sex slaves in Thailand, and they are denied education in India. Yet most of us westerners are oblivious to this cruel injustice. It's out of sight, out of mind.

But in 2009 a movie that exposed the cruel abuse of women in Iran hit theaters just a few weeks after Iran's authoritarian government came under international scrutiny. *The Stoning of Soraya M.* is based on a book written by French-Iranian journalist Freidoune Sahebjam.[7] It tells the true story of a woman named Zahra, who is distraught because the men of her village—she defiantly calls them "devils"—have killed her niece, Soraya.[8]

Through flashbacks we learn that Soraya's immoral husband decided to put her away so he could marry a fourteen-year-old girl. When Soraya dares to defy her husband's scheme, he trumps up false adultery charges against her with the help of the local Islamic mullah. Zahra tries to stop the madness, but in the end the villagers commit

13

the Islamic version of a lynching. Along the way we learn how militant the antiwoman attitudes are in this part of the world.

"Women now have no voices," Zahra says at one point. We see
how Iran's women, under the regime of the Ayatollah Khomeini, were
forced to live in prisons of silence and were valued only as sex objects
and domestic servants.

The worst part of the movie's twenty-minute stoning sequence is
the way young men in the village click their rocks together while they
wait for the signal to kill.

Why does this kind of madness still happen in the twenty-first
century? I have seen it up close since I began confronting the abuse
of women in 2001. I've traveled to more than twenty-four countries
to conduct conferences and seminars, and I have interviewed many
"Zahras" from every continent. I now carry a heavy burden for these
women, and for the men who abuse them. Here are just a few of the
statistics we know about this ignored issue.

1. Around the world, at least one in three women will be
   beaten, coerced into sex, or otherwise abused during her
   lifetime.[9]

2. In Latin America, the culture of *machismo,* or institu-
   tionalized male pride, has resulted in a dangerously low
   view of women. A report released in 2009 by the United
   Nations says up to 40 percent of women throughout Latin
   America have been victims of physical violence.[10]

3. Forced prostitution, trafficking for sex, and sex tourism
   are growing problems in many parts of the world. Each
   year, an estimated 800,000 people are trafficked across
   borders. Eighty percent of these are women and girls,
   according to the United Nations Population Fund
   (UNPF). Most of them end up trapped in the commercial
   sex trade. (This figure does not include the substantial

number of women and girls who are bought and sold within their own countries.)[11]

4. According to the UNPF, the greatest number of victims is believed to come from Asia (about 250,000 per year), the former Soviet Union (about 100,000), and from Central and Eastern Europe (about 175,000).[12] An estimated 100,000 trafficked women have come from Latin America and the Caribbean, with more than 50,000 from Africa.[13]

5. In Asia, at least sixty million girls are "missing" due to prenatal sex selection, infanticide, or neglect.[14] In China, where young couples are only allowed to have one child, orphanages are overrun with infant girls, because boys are preferred. Baby girls are often thrown into rivers, left on doorsteps, or abandoned in forests.

6. Female genital mutilation affects an estimated 130 million women and girls, mostly in Africa. Each year, two million more undergo the barbaric practice.[15] In most cases, a girl is forced around age twelve to undergo the cutting away of her clitoris so that she cannot feel sexual pleasure. Often this causes serious urinary problems as well as infections.

7. Violence against women also takes the form of other harmful practices, such as child marriage and dowry-related violence (especially in India), acid burning (in some Muslim nations), and abandonment of widows.[16]

8. In many Islamic countries, women die from what is known as "honor killings." If a woman dares to disagree with her husband or even shows a hint of disrespect, her husband and other male relatives (and sometimes her mother) will drag her into the street, bury her up to her waist in dirt, and then stone her in broad daylight.

Although this practice is illegal, it is estimated that there are five thousand such killings every year.[17]

9. Guatemala has the highest rate of unsolved murders of women in the world. A report released in 2005 by Amnesty International showed that murders of women climbed to 560 in that year, yet not one murderer was convicted. In many cases, the women victims are tortured or their bodies are mutilated. Often their bodies are dumped in the streets.[18]

10. In South Africa, older men who have contracted the AIDS virus believe that if they have sex with a young virgin they will be cured of the disease.[19] So they actually search for young girls to serve as their "wives," and they buy them from their poor parents. Needless to say, many of these innocent girls do not survive.

It's easy to read statistics like this and just push them aside. After all, we don't know these people, and we feel powerless to help them. But after I began traveling and speaking on this issue I began to match actual names and faces with these abstract numbers. Suddenly I began to feel the personal pain of the women and girls involved. Because I am a husband and the father of four daughters, I began to see these abused women in a different light. I identified with them. And my heart broke.

In Kochi, India, a desperate woman came to a house where I was having lunch. She was afraid to talk to me, so she spoke with the pastor's wife, who was hosting our meal. This woman's husband had just dragged her to a river and dunked her under the water repeatedly. He threatened to drown her until she promised to go to her parents and request more dowry money. She was risking her life to talk about the abuse because most women in India suffer silently. They consider it disrespectful to discuss family problems openly.

In Kampala, Uganda, a nineteen-year-old college student asked if she could meet with me in the church along with her pastor. Because I openly talked about sex abuse in a sermon, she mustered the courage to share her shameful secret: two male cousins had violated her when she was only thirteen. They took her to the countryside and told her they were going to ride horses, but when they arrived at their destination, both boys raped her repeatedly. When she threatened to tell their parents, one boy retorted, "They will never believe you. Girls are always the guilty ones."

In Port Harcourt, Nigeria, I met a twenty-four-year-old woman who came to me in tears. Her Christian father and mother had a happy family of four daughters. Yet her father decided to divorce his wife after all the girls were grown. The reason? Because this woman had not given him a son. "Nigerian men think it is the wife's duty to give them a boy," the distraught daughter explained. "They don't even realize it is the sperm of the man that determines the gender of the child."

In Nairobi, Kenya, a tired-looking woman asked me for prayer at the altar of a church. She had not been sleeping much. She said her husband regularly visited prostitutes, but sometimes he also demanded sex from her even though she was afraid he would infect her with the AIDS virus. Often he forced himself on her anyway; if she locked the bedroom door, he kicked it open.

In Kiev, Ukraine—a city known for its mafia-run prostitution rings—I spoke to a conference of three thousand women about the healing Jesus Christ offers to victims of sex abuse. When I opened the altars for women to receive prayer, almost every woman in the auditorium tried to crowd to the front. A Ukrainian woman later told me, "Most women here have been abused like that."

In La Paz, Bolivia, I spent many days ministering to the poor, indigenous people of that nation. I saw countless women on the streets of the city selling candy, cigarettes, stationery, and soft drinks from small wooden stands while their young children crawled on the dirty sidewalks or sat on mats behind their crude kiosks. The women's husbands were nowhere to be found. I later learned that many Bolivian men force their wives to work in the streets while they stay home all day to drink alcohol. These women have a popular saying that everyone in Bolivia knows by heart: "*Cuanto más me pega, más me ama.*" This means, "The more [my husband] beats me, the more he loves me."

And in Monterrey, Mexico, an articulate woman pastor pulled me aside after I had spoken about domestic violence at a conference. She wanted to tell me the unthinkable. "Every month I go to the hospital to visit a pastor's wife," she whispered, as if she was afraid someone might overhear. "Pastors are beating their wives. The problem is not just in the secular culture. It is also in the church!"

After hearing these kinds of stories from women all over the world, I decided I could not sit on my hands or close my ears. I went on the warpath against the oppression of women. I began to write about it, preach about it, and mobilize churches to confront it. I sponsored women's conferences, men's conferences, and pastor's conferences so I could hit the issue from all sides.

I also realized that this violence won't stop until men forcefully oppose it. I now believe that this is one mark of a true man: he stands up against all forms of social oppression—including this horrible sin of abuse and gender discrimination. Real men don't put down women. Real men fight for them. Our mothers, sisters, and daughters need us to speak out. They have suffered long enough.

Let's Talk About It

1. Were you already aware of this problem of violence against women? How did you learn about it?
2. How do these statistics about gender-based violence make you feel?
3. Is there something you can do to address this problem in your own church, community, or elsewhere?

A BIBLICAL VIEW OF GENDER

One of the main reasons there is such pervasive violence against women is that men believe they are superior. We have several terms for this attitude. Some call it *chauvinism*, a word derived from the name of a French soldier, Nicolas Chauvin, who was fanatically loyal to Napoleon Bonaparte. Napoleon himself was the ultimate chauvinist. He once said, "Nature intended women to be our slaves. They are our property."

In Latin America, this attitude is called *machismo*, and it is promoted not only by authoritarian men but also by women who teach their sons that they are superior to women. Chauvinism is also known as a patriarchal mind-set—and it includes the idea that only men can lead and that women were created only to have babies and serve men.

Ultimately, male pride has its roots in the Garden of Eden, where Adam and Eve disobeyed God and the world came under the curse of sin. Before the Fall, Adam and Eve enjoyed a perfect, intimate partnership without any shame or dysfunction in their relationship. After the Fall, the man began to dominate the woman, and her life became more painful. Adam blamed his wife for being deceived, even though he willingly chose to rebel against God. The Lord said this to the woman in Genesis 3:16:

> To the woman He said, "I will greatly multiply your pain in childbirth, in pain you will bring forth children; yet your desire will be for your husband, and he will rule over you."

You don't have to look far to see Genesis 3:16 at work in the world. In every culture on Earth, especially those where the gospel of Jesus Christ has never been preached, women suffer under the domination of men.

If you examine the world's religions, you will find that all of them except Christianity denigrate women and place them at severe disadvantage. In Islamic cultures, especially where Sharia law is enforced, women have no civil rights and are not even allowed to drive cars. In Hindu cultures, women suffer unimaginable discrimination; for centuries, in fact, a Hindu wife whose husband died was expected to commit suicide by jumping into his funeral pyre. In Mormonism, women whose "celestial marriages" are sealed in temple ceremonies are told that the only way they can attain eternal salvation is if they have babies.

Christianity offers a unique and revolutionary message of empowerment to women, and the Bible calls men to treat women as equals. Jesus Christ, who showed amazing compassion to women during His earthly ministry and who called women to be His followers, canceled the painful reality of Genesis 3:16. I like to preach that Genesis 3:16 was canceled by John 3:16! When Christ came into the world as the Father's only begotten Son to save us, He made a way for men to be delivered from their pride and for women to be healed from violence and abuse.

Of course, Christian leaders themselves have not always walked in total deliverance from male pride. The church has not always reflected the heart of Christ. Some leaders, even today, impose their own gender biases and errant interpretations of Scripture—and this has led to much pain in the lives of Christian women around the world. That's why it is so important for us to go back to Scripture and recover what the Bible actually says on this issue, rather than parroting religious traditions that were passed down to us.

Here are seven important truths about gender that have been clearly articulated in Scripture. You must allow the Word of God to renew your mind. These principles will help liberate you from the heavy yoke of male pride.

1. Men and women were created by God with equal value.

The first account of Creation in Genesis 1 says God created both the male and the female in the divine image. Genesis 1:26–27 says:

Then God said, "Let Us make man in Our image, according to Our likeness; and let them rule over the fish of the sea and over the birds of the sky and over the cattle and over all the earth, and over every creeping thing that creeps on the earth." God created man in His own image, in the image of God He created him; male and female He created them.

In ancient Greece, philosophers such as Aristotle and others believed the male was created from the divine matter of the gods, while the female was created from inferior animal matter. The Judeo-Christian view of gender is in stark contrast to the pagan Greek mind-set. In the very first chapter in the Bible we see that men and women are created as equals.

The word picture that is painted in this passage is of two equal partners standing side by side. Then, in the Genesis 2 description of Eve's creation, we are told that she was taken from Adam's side. It is worth noting that God did not take the woman from his head (so that she would rule over him) or from his feet (so that he would rule over her). God's intention for marriage was always for intimacy, affection, and partnership.

2. In their original perfection, the man and woman were both given authority.

Even some Christians believe that women can never have spiritual authority. Yet throughout Scripture, in both Old and New Testaments, we see that God anointed certain women with leadership gifts. Genesis 1:28 says:

God blessed them; and God said to them, "Be fruitful and multiply, and fill the earth, and *subdue* it; and rule over the fish of the sea and over the birds of the sky and over every living thing that moves on the earth."

The word *subdue* in this passage is the Hebrew word *kabash*, which means "to subdue, dominate, tread down." Women are called to do this also! This was always God's plan: that men and women would rule together to advance His kingdom.

Of course, Adam and Eve's fall in the Garden of Eden created a huge setback. But when Christ came and paid the full price for our sins, He made full restoration possible. Now, because of His redemption, men *and* women can walk in divine authority once more.

3. God never intended for women to be viewed as appendages or as servants to men.

The woman is referred to in Genesis 2:18 as the man's "helper" (or "help meet" in the King James Version). What does that word mean? If we have chauvinism in our hearts, we might be tempted to believe that God gave the woman to Adam simply so she could pick up his socks, fix his dinner, and meet his sexual needs whenever he pleased.

But actually the word *helper* does not imply subservience or inferiority. If anything, the passage shows that the man was totally incomplete without the woman—and that he could not fulfill his divine mission without her. The passage says:

> Then the LORD God said, "It is not good for the man to be alone; I will make him a helper suitable for him."

This word *helper* comes from the Hebrew word *ezer*, a term that actually refers to God more than fifteen times in the Old Testament! Of course we know that God is our helper, but we would never think of Him as inferior to us. Neither should we think of women as inferior or second-class just because Eve was created after Adam. (After all, Adam was created after God made all the animals, but we don't consider man inferior to animals!)

4. God does not value boys over girls, so neither should we.

In many cultures in the world girls are at a huge disadvantage. In India, for example, many families choose abortion if an ultrasound shows the unborn baby is female. In many cultures males are considered more valuable because they will grow up and be more financially productive. But this is not how God views girls.

In the Book of Numbers, we read about five women who were the daughters of a man named Zelophehad. This man had died with no male heirs, and the traditions of Israel said that a man with only daughters would leave no land rights to his family. However, when these women came to Moses to protest, Moses asked God what to do. Numbers 27:6–7 says:

> Then the LORD spoke to Moses, saying, "The daughters of Zelophehad are right in their statements. You shall surely give them a hereditary possession among their father's brothers, and you shall transfer the inheritance of their father to them."

That one moment changed the course of life among the children of Israel. God contradicted the patriarchal traditions of the day and ruled in favor of the daughters of Zelophehad. He made it clear that women do indeed have equal value in His eyes.

5. Jesus Christ modeled a completely different approach to women than that of the religious leaders of His time.

When He began His ministry, Jesus challenged the religious and cultural rules of a male-dominated culture. While other rabbis believed it was improper to teach women the Bible, Jesus called his disciple Mary to sit at His feet. While other religious leaders refused to go near bleeding women, Jesus healed one. While the Pharisees shunned Samaritans and divorced women, Jesus had compassion on the Samaritan divorcée and commissioned her to be an evangelist.

Jesus's approach to ministry was radical for His time. If a Jewish leader saw a woman coming down the street, he would typically get on the other side of the street to avoid her. Yet Jesus went out of His way to befriend women, even those who were the outcasts of society. He also allowed a group of women to travel with His entourage (Luke 8:1–3), and those same women became the first witnesses of His resurrection—in a time when women were not even allowed to testify in a court of law

6. The New Testament calls men to treat women as equals.

In the first century, marriage was a painful prison for most women. Husbands viewed their wives as property. Women had no right to seek a divorce, and there was no protection from violence. Yet to this male-dominated culture the apostle Paul wrote the epistle to the Ephesians, which contains the most revolutionary description of marriage ever penned. Paul explains that marriage is not a hierarchy but a partnership that celebrates equality, tender intimacy, and unity of heart. He gave husbands these instructions in Ephesians 5:25 and 28:

> Husbands, love your wives, just as Christ also loved the church and gave Himself up for her. . . . So husbands ought also to love their own wives as their own bodies. He who loves his own wife loves himself.

Paul also challenged the Corinthian church with another radical idea about marriage. He told them that men and women have equal authority over each other's bodies when it comes to sex. This concept cut deep at the heart of a patriarchal culture, because men believed they had the right to demand sex from their wives whenever they wanted. Paul said:

> The husband must fulfill his duty to his wife, and likewise also the wife to her husband. The wife does not have authority over her own body, but the husband does; and likewise also the husband does not have authority over his own body, but the wife does.
>
> —1 CORINTHIANS 7:3–4

This passage offers the essence of New Testament teaching on marriage. Clearly, if God desires an attitude of mutual submission and equality in the sexual area, which lies at the very core of a man and woman's relationship, then He also desires that husbands and wives treat each other with the same attitude in every other area of life.

7. The Holy Spirit empowers both men and women for ministry.

When the Holy Spirit was poured out on the early church on the Day of Pentecost, both the male and female followers of Christ were together in the Upper Room. The Bible says a flame of God's fire rested on each person. It does not say that the men had blue flames, while the women had pink flames. The same holy power came upon men and women alike.

After that dramatic encounter, both men and women began to preach the gospel with power. Philip the evangelist had four daughters who were prophets (Acts 21:9). A married couple, Priscilla and Aquila, traveled with Paul and taught the Word of God (Acts 18:24–26). Paul commended a woman minister named Phoebe because she was a powerful deacon of the church (Rom. 16:1–2).

Throughout Paul's writings he makes it clear that the gifts of the Holy Spirit are not given to people based on gender, race, or financial status. God anoints whomever He wills. Nowhere in Scripture are spiritual gifts linked to gender. In fact, Paul told the Galatians:

> There is neither Jew nor Greek, there is neither slave nor free man, there is neither male nor female; for you are all one in Christ Jesus.
>
> —GALATIANS 3:28

Under the old covenant, only Jewish males from the tribe of Levi who were between the ages of twenty-five and fifty could serve as priests in the tabernacle. But all that changed after Jesus came. Because of His death on the cross and because of the outpouring of the Holy Spirit at Pentecost, all restrictions related to age, class, race, and gender were removed. Today, Christ has a new "holy priesthood" (1 Pet. 2:9) that is made up of both men and women from every language, tribe, and nation.

Let's Talk About It

1. How do you explain why there is so much violence and abuse toward women in the world? Is there a spiritual root to this issue?
2. What did God mean when He called Eve a "helper"? Have you ever treated your wife, or women in general, as inferior?
3. What do you think it means to love your wife "as Christ loves the church"?
4. Secular feminists sometimes angrily demand women's rights and use crude language to describe men. How does this form of angry feminism differ from a biblical view of gender equality?
5. The apostle Paul had many women on his ministry team, such as Phoebe, Priscilla, Euodia, and Syntyche. Yet he seemed to limit women at times, such as when he told them to be quiet in church (1 Cor. 14:34–35). How do you explain that?

Let's Pray About It

Father, I don't want any chauvinism or male pride in my heart. Please break my hard heart. Forgive me for any time I have mistreated my wife or other women. I want to have the heart of Christ, who showed respect, dignity, and compassion for women and recognized their equality. In Jesus's name, amen.

My father? I never knew him. Never even seen a picture of him.[1]
—RAPPER EMINEM

*My father was a management genius. But
what I really wanted was a dad.*[2]
—POP SINGER MICHAEL JACKSON

Ninety percent of men on death row hate their father.[3]
—DAVE SIMMONS, AUTHOR, *DAD, THE FAMILY COUNSELOR*

I never knew my father, but the old TV was always there for me.[4]
—JIM CARREY AS "CHIP DOUGLAS" IN *THE CABLE GUY*

*I never knew my father; he bailed out before I was born. I don't
even know his name, which is why I have these tattoos. This
one means "Father" (points to right side of neck) and this one
means "Death" (left side of neck). It used to bother me a lot, and
then I was like "[Forget] it, I'm not going to dwell on it."*[5]
—COREY TAYLOR, VOCALIST FOR THE METAL BAND SLIPKNOT

10 LIES

A MAN CANNOT BE CLOSE TO HIS FATHER.

P EOPLE JOKED ABOUT Jack Frost's name, but there was absolutely nothing cold about the guy. Though his fans loved his teachings, what they remember most about him was his warm hug.

Whenever the popular Bible teacher would finish his lengthy sermons, he always invited people to the altar to receive what he called "a baptism of the Father's love." He and other members of his ministry team would face the audience, and seekers would form lines to receive a lengthy embrace.

Worshipers would linger in the church for hours to "soak" in God's presence after listening to Jack's message. Men hugged men, and women hugged women while a worship team played soft music in the background. There was nothing sexual about these moments. It was as if the love of God became tangible. Sometimes grown men in their sixties would sob like babies while Jack wrapped his burly arms around them.

I am glad I was one of the people who got a hug from Jack before he died prematurely in 2007 at the age of fifty-four after a tough battle with cancer. He left behind a rich spiritual legacy, recorded in his books and deposited in the many people he trained at Shiloh Place, his ministry base near Myrtle Beach, South Carolina.

Houston Miles, a pastor who served with Jack for many years, told me the week of his funeral, "Everywhere Jack preached, the altars were full of people who didn't get the love they needed growing up. He accomplished more in ten years than most people accomplish in a lifetime."

Jack Frost's message was as simple as it was profound. He used his own life experiences—including his failures and weaknesses—to show people that God's unconditional love can heal the effects of neglect, abuse, abandonment, shame, and rejection. As a practical theologian and as a counselor, he understood the human heart and its deepest need for acceptance and approval.

Guys found it easy to relate to Jack, a rugged man's man who spent years of his life sailing boats off the coast of the southeastern United States and earning the coveted title of "Top Hook." He openly talked about his dysfunctional relationship with his own performance-oriented father and how that struggle caused him to view God as distant, strict, and legalistic.

Jack's passion was to help Christians renounce distorted views of God so they could know His intimacy and affection. In his first book, *Experiencing the Father's Embrace*, he used scientific research to prove that human beings need love in order to thrive. "Scientists have actually proven that humans are four to seven times more likely to succumb to sickness if they do not have a normal dose of nurturing love," he wrote.[6]

Jack decided in 1993 that he would begin dispensing that divine love in mega-doses. With his wife, Trisha, he created Shiloh Place as a haven for burned-out ministers and anyone else who needed emotional healing. He shared his message in conferences and training seminars for more than fifteen years.

In the summer of 2001 I traveled with Jack to Toronto, Canada, on a ministry trip—mainly to help him outline his first book. After listening to him for five days, his teachings on the Father's love saturated my soul and became a part of my own life message. In fact, there have been times when I have modeled my own ministry after Jack's and have asked people to come to the altar for a healing embrace, especially men who never knew the approval of their own dads.

The week before Jack's funeral I held a young Chinese man in my arms at the altar of a church in Singapore. After I asked the Holy Spirit to reveal the depth of God's love to him, I pulled back and realized that the whole right side of my shirt was wet with tears. I thought of Jack Frost and how he taught me that the love of God is not just a doctrine or a philosophy. It is a tangible commodity that flows from the Holy Spirit through His people to those who are starving to know they have worth and value.

KNOWING GOD AS YOUR FATHER

The apostle John spoke more about our relationship with the Father than any other biblical writer. There are 112 references to God as "Father" in John's Gospel (compared to 44 in Matthew, 5 in Mark, and 14 in Luke) and another 17 references to the Father in John's epistles.

I have often pondered why John talked so much about the fatherhood of God and why he seemed to understand better than any other disciple that Jesus Christ was the embodiment of the Father on Earth. John quoted Jesus saying, "I and my Father are one" (John 10:30, KJV), and "Believe Me that I am in the Father and the Father is in Me" (John 14:11). John not only understood that Jesus was God, but He also had a deep revelation of how much God, who was in Christ, is a perfect Father.

John referred to himself as "the disciple whom Jesus loved" (John 13:23, NIV). This is why John is sometimes referred to as Jesus's best friend. It does not mean Jesus loved John more than His other disciples, but it does imply that John perhaps understood the love of the Savior at a deeper level. Why is that?

The Bible does not tell us. We certainly don't know much about John's home life. It is possible that John did not have a good relationship with his own father—and that Jesus actually came to fulfill that role in his life as a true spiritual father. Perhaps it was John's deep need for a loving father that caused him to follow Christ so passionately. Perhaps it is why He was even willing to stand at the cross of Calvary when Jesus was dying—while all the other male disciples had fled from the Roman soldiers and Jewish leaders.

And it might even offer the reason why John was privileged to have the "last word" by writing the last book of the Bible—the Book of Revelation. One thing is for certain: if you know God's love in a deeply personal way, that perfect love will change you. The apostle John's theme is best summarized in 1 John 3:1:

> See how great a love the Father has bestowed upon us, that we would be called children of God.

We are exhorted to open our heart and stretch our imagination to comprehend the amazing love of our heavenly Father. His love is truly unfathomable (Eph. 3:8), yet John and other New Testament writers exhort us to at least try to measure its length, width, height, and depth. The Bible is a virtual gold mine of revelation about the Father's great love. It tells us:

- The Father knows our needs even before we ask for them, and He longs to provide for us (Matt. 6:8). He is overwhelmingly generous to His children.
- The Father is eager to forgive His wayward children if they will simply come back to fellowship with Him (Luke 15:11–24). He does not hold grudges against us. He is totally accepting of us despite our failures.

- The Father seeks out people to be His worshipers (John 4:23). In other words, He desires intimate fellowship with us. He pursues us, even when we are in rebellion against Him.

- The Father will draw close to anyone who believes in His Son, Jesus (John 16:23). He abides with us in a covenant relationship, and He promises never to abandon us.

- He is called "the Father of mercies and God of all comfort" (2 Cor. 1:3), which means He is quick to forgive our mistakes, console us in difficult times, and restore us if we have failed. Although He is strong, He is also tender and sympathetic.

- God places a cry inside of us that says, "Abba, Father" (Gal. 4:6). This means that God Himself places a need for His love in our souls. He wants us to relate to Him as a child to a father.

- The Father and the Son are in a perfect relationship, and they invite us to join in their fellowship (1 John 1:3). God is not selfish about His love. He is eager to share it with all of us.

For many men today, however, the word *father* hits a raw nerve. It does not conjure up good feelings. Many men suffer from what has been termed "the father ache." Many guys have a deep void in their souls because their dads failed them in one way or another. Fathers were intended to equip us for life by giving us these things:

1. Strong, masculine affection to make us secure and emotionally healthy. (This includes verbal affirmation as well as nonverbal affection.)

2. Protection so we can grow up to be fearless risk-takers.

3. Guidance and counsel to help us develop godly wisdom and make right choices about life, finances, career, marriage, and family.

4. Loving discipline so we can know our moral boundaries.

5. Unconditional approval and encouragement so we can fulfill our God-given assignments.

6. Generous provision so we will not only be blessed, but we will also be a blessing to others.

Without a father's blessing, a man will feel like less than a man. The lack of a loving father leaves a hollow place in our heart. It can lead some men down the path toward drug or alcohol addiction because they want to numb the pain. Guys who never sensed their father's approval can become stressed-out, driven workaholics who desperately try to prove to their value to everyone else. Men whose fathers are poor moral examples often will choose a life of immorality.

Men who never experienced a father's discipline often are drawn into violence and crime and sometimes end up in prison. And men who never experienced any physical affection from their fathers sometimes develop homosexual leanings—all because their boyhood need to be held in a dad's strong arms was never met.

Many men even grow up to hate their fathers because of the way they failed them. And this family breakdown ends up being perpetuated from one generation to the next. The very last passage in the Old Testament speaks about this generational breakdown. It says in Malachi 4:5–6:

> Behold, I am going to send you Elijah the prophet before the coming of the great and terrible day of the LORD. He will restore the hearts of the fathers to their children and the hearts of the children to their fathers, so that I will not come and smite the land with a curse.

The reference to Elijah in this promise speaks of Jesus Christ, who offered the only solution to the tragic rift between fathers and sons. It is only through Christ that fathers can fulfill their duties to their sons, and it is only through Christ that wounded sons can find the grace to forgive their fathers for their failures. Jesus offers the only true path to the healing of the father wound.

Let's Talk About It

1. When you think of your own father, what words first come to mind? How would you honestly describe him?
2. If you are now a father, how do you feel your parenting style differs from that of your own father's? If you aren't yet a father, how would you like your parenting style to differ from your father's?
3. Study the list of the six duties of a father mentioned earlier. Which of these did your father do best? Explain why.
4. Describe a time when you felt especially close to your father, either as a child or an adult. Why was this time so special?

HEALING THE FATHER WOUND

Christian counselors often use the phrase "father wound" to describe the pain we feel because of what our fathers either did wrong or neglected to do for us. These wounds can be especially painful if we experienced any form of abuse during our formative years. If you had a decent father who loved your mother, provided a roof over your head, kept you well fed, and even came to your football games, band performances, or graduation ceremonies in high school, then you are among a minority of men who grew up in an intact family. Many, many guys did not have that blessing.

For years church leaders, educators, and sociologists have been warning Americans about the alarming erosion of the family in the United States. Here are just a few of the grim statistics:

- The decline of marriage has been the single most important demographic change in the United States since the end of World War II, according to a study of the breakdown of the family conducted by Dr. Michael Rendall of the College of Human Ecology at Cornell University.[7]
- In 1960 there were seventy-four marriages for every one thousand unmarried women and nine divorces for every one thousand married women. By 1991, there were just fifty-four marriages per one thousand unmarried women and twenty-one divorces per one thousand married women. The marriage rate dropped a full 25 percent, while the divorce rate increased by 230 percent.[8]
- The United States today has the highest divorce rate in the entire world. Half of all first marriages in this country end in divorce, and the mortality rate of second marriages is even higher.
- More than a million children each year become the innocent victims of divorce.
- In 2010, about 40 percent of American children were born out of wedlock.[9]

These statistics, of course, highlight only the problem of fatherlessness. Many other problems lurk under the surface in families with dysfunctional fathers. What type of father did you have? He may fit in one of the following categories.

1. The disciplinarian father

Some men grow up in families where the father is harsh, strict, and demanding. He may be this way because he has big aspirations for his children. But by requiring such high standards (for example, perfect moral behavior, high grades, or superiority in sports), the father clearly implies that his love for his son is conditional. Depending on the personality of the son, this type of performance-oriented parenting can either crush a boy or turn him into a rebel.

In the 1989 movie *Dead Poets Society*, a teenager named Neil Perry is sent to an exclusive private school for boys by his overbearing father—who hopes his son will follow in his footsteps as a doctor.[10] But Neil's nonconformist English teacher, Mr. Keating, encourages him to try out for the school play, and the boy discovers he loves Shakespeare. He ends up in the role of Puck in *A Midsummer Night's Dream*.

The story ends in tragedy when Neil's father threatens to pull him out of school—all because he does not want his son to explore a career path he doesn't approve of. What Neil wanted most was his dad's approval, and he hoped his dad would applaud his performance in the play. What he gets from his father is a constant barrage of scowls, browbeating, threats, and lectures. The negativity is so painful to Neil that he ends up shooting himself with a gun he finds in his father's desk.

This is only a fictional example, but when a father's love has conditions attached to it, his son will battle all kinds of emotions, including anger, self-loathing, and insecurity. A son who is starved for his father's approval will spend the rest of his life looking for it from other people.

2. The passive father

While the disciplinarian is too strict and demanding, a passive father is at the other end of the spectrum. He may be in the house every day, but he never offers his son advice, counsel, or correction. Sometimes this happens when the father has a long-term illness or some kind of serious emotional problem. But some otherwise healthy fathers find themselves incapable of providing the strong, protective discipline that every son needs.

Psychologists have proven that children feel much more protected when they are given clear boundaries. If they are allowed to run wild, they become nervous, insecure, and fearful, as well as rowdy and erratic. God designed us with a need for moral limitations, and our parents have the responsibility to provide this through loving discipline.

When children are small, they require physical discipline in the form of spankings. Some modern behaviorists theorize that spanking a child will lead him or her to become violent, but I have seen the opposite. When a father uses physical punishment in a loving way with his son, positive behavioral change always follows.

Discipline should always be administered carefully. When I spanked my young daughters, I always took them into their rooms and talked to them privately first. I never spanked them in front of others to create embarrassment. I explained to them what they had done wrong and why it was necessary for me to correct them. Then I swatted them a few times with a small ruler or wooden spoon. They cried, but after their punishment I always held them in my arms and reassured them that Daddy loved them.

Every child needs this kind of loving correction. If a father is wimpish, lenient, or nonchalant about his children's behavior, he will pay for it later. In addition, a son who is never disciplined by his father will eventually resent him for letting him run wild.

3. The abusive father

My friend Medad is a pastor from the East African country of Uganda. If you met him today, you would think he is one of most loving, emotionally balanced men you'd ever met. That's why I was so shocked to learn of the horrors he experienced when he was growing up with his tyrannical father.

Medad's mother had five daughters before she became pregnant with him. But like many Ugandan men, Medad's father did not want girl children. He was angry because his wife kept giving birth to girls. When Medad was in his mother's womb, his father kicked and beat his wife seven times to cause a miscarriage—but miraculously Medad was born without complications.

After his birth, Medad's mother had four more daughters—and this made Medad's father even angrier. To punish his wife he married five more wives and had a total of thirty-two children. (Polygamy is legal and quite common in parts of Uganda.) As the father grew older and faced financial difficulties, he became more and more violent. He often beat Medad with the same stick he used to hit his first wife. Today Medad still bears the scars of those beatings all over his chest, back, and stomach.

When Medad became a teenager, the father decided to punish his first wife and her children. He told his wife she was the cause of all of his problems—and then he drove her, Medad, and his sisters into a rural area and abandoned them on the side of a road. Before driving away, he picked up some ashes out of a bucket and pronounced a curse on all of them. "This is your inheritance," the father said as he threw a handful of ashes into the air. "I am not leaving you land, houses, or money. May you blow away and become nothing, just like this dust."

From that moment, Medad felt nothing but intense hatred for his father. In high school he got involved in violent gang activity, and he planned to join the military so he could get his own gun. He wanted to kill his father, his father's other wives, and all other people who had made his life miserable. Thankfully that is not how the story ended. Medad met Jesus Christ when he was in college, and the first thing he did after his conversion was forgive his father from his heart. Many years later, after his mother and many of his sisters became Christians, they all had a glorious reconciliation.

But not all stories of abuse have such happy endings. If your father was physically, emotionally, or sexually abusive, you may still carry deep scars. You may also carry a heavy load of guilt, because children who are abused often blame themselves for their parents' actions.

4. The emotionally distant father

In many cultures men do not feel a freedom to laugh, cry, or express love openly. They are taught to stuff their emotions inside—usually because their fathers tell them that showing any form of emotion, except anger, is a sign of weakness. As these men grow older, they become almost like wooden statues. They actually lose the ability to feel compassion, joy, or sadness.

You can see this phenomenon in some European countries. It may not be an accurate stereotype, but Germans, Swedes, Norwegians, and British men, among others, are often characterized as being stoic. Sometimes churches encourage this attitude, especially in more intellectual environments. That's why many Christian men are raised in homes where their fathers seem detached and uninvolved in the lives of their children.

An emotionally distant father may truly love his son, but he feels powerless to express that love. He does not feel the freedom to wrestle with him on the floor, tussle his hair, tickle his ribs, swing him in the air, or kiss him on the cheek at bedtime, nor does he have the capacity to say, "I love you," or "Daddy is so proud of you."

The lack of physical affection, combined with the absence of any verbal affirmation, creates a gap that grows when the boy becomes a teenager. Before long the generation gap becomes a chasm that widens every year until the father and son hardly communicate at all. Their relationship is reduced to infrequent telephone calls on Father's Day or superficial conversations about sports and the weather.

Sons who do not receive any real display of love from their fathers feel deprived and may grow to resent their fathers. They also may grow up with the same inability to show their emotions.

5. The absentee father

The 2009 movie *The Blind Side* is the true story of Michael Oher, a fatherless, African American boy from Memphis, Tennessee, who grew up to become a legendary offensive tackle for the Baltimore

Ravens football team.[11] After a wealthy white woman named Leigh Anne Tuohy learns that "Big Mike" is homeless, she invites him to stay with her husband and two children in their immaculate suburban home. Eventually the Tuohy family adopts Michael and helps him improve his grades so he can play football for his high school team.

The Blind Side was one of the most uplifting films in recent memory, but it also accurately portrayed the pain that torments so many men who did not have fathers in the home. In Mike Oher's case, he did not even know who his father was until a high school principal tells him that he's dead. And when Leigh Anne Tuohy pays a visit to Mike's crack-addicted mother, the woman struggles even to remember Mike's father's name.

For Mike Oher, and for thousands of other guys like him, an absentee father means poverty and neglect. It also creates feelings of abandonment, isolation, and a loss of identity. Many guys from single-parent homes feel God has abandoned them, causing them to question their own worth and value.

6. The addicted father

My friend Paul (not his real name) has been a pastor for almost thirty years. He has a wonderful wife, two children, and a great sense of humor. The members of his church appreciate his mature spiritual leadership. But like so many of us, this man has a dark side. He struggles with deep insecurity and feelings of rejection. When I asked him to pinpoint the root of his problems, he began to share memories of his father.

Paul is particularly haunted by some words his dad said when he was only seven years old. Paul was with his sister in the backseat of the family car when his dad got in, motioned to the scraggly boy, and said gruffly, "Does *he* have to come?" Paul's parents talked for a while, then his father asked Paul to go inside the house. He stayed home alone all day while the rest of his family visited with friends.

Years later when Paul asked some Christian friends to pray for him about this incident, he had to process years of his father's belittling and abusive behavior. Sometimes the comments were subtle. His father sometimes gave a scowling look of disgust that meant, "You can't do anything right." Other times he would slap Paul or his brother on the ears for no reason.

The children in this family rarely spoke at the dinner table when their father was present. They feared him. Sometimes Paul's dad would poke his son's hand with a fork if he did something wrong. Once his father made Paul sit outside on a porch in subfreezing weather to punish him. It was not until Paul was fourteen that he learned the painful secret that his mother had hidden from him: his father had been an alcoholic ever since he had returned from military service in World War II.

Paul told me, "I didn't know my dad drank, so I internalized all the pain as though it were my fault. I learned the truth when my oldest brother brought my drunken dad home from his workplace. My dad was smashed out of his mind, and my mother dragged him into the living room in front of my two younger siblings and me and asked him, 'Is that any way to come home to your children?' I'm sure my mother was the biggest victim of it all."

The saddest part of Paul's familiar story isn't what his dad did to him or said to him. It is what he did *not* do and what he did *not* say. The man never hugged his son, tussled his hair, or kissed him on the cheek. There was no affection whatsoever. And he never once said, "I love you," to the love-starved boy.

Amazingly, Paul's story does not end with tragedy. He became a Christian and eventually went into the ministry, and he has helped hundreds of people experience the love of God. And several years later, his father had a life-changing encounter with Christ and was delivered from his alcohol addiction. Paul can truly say today that the cruel father who once said, "Does *he* have to come?" is a transformed man.

Our fathers often help shape the way we view God, either good or bad. If you had any of these types of dysfunctional fathers, you may also struggle because you think God is this way. You must remember:

- Your father may have been a strict disciplinarian, but your heavenly Father does not base His love on your performance. He loves you even when you fail.

- Your father may have been passive and weak, and he may have withheld discipline from you. But your heavenly Father loves you enough to correct you. In fact, the Bible says in Hebrews 12:6, "For those whom the Lord loves He disciplines, and He scourges every son whom He receives."

- Your earthly father may have been abusive. He may have beaten you mercilessly, neglected you, or even sexually abused you. But your heavenly Father is not an abuser. He is a protector, and He actually brings justice to those who have been abused.

- Your father may have been emotionally distant, but God does not withhold His love. He is full of encouragement, joyful praise, and loving encouragement. When you get to know your heavenly Father, you will discover that He always has something positive to say to you, and He is eager to lavish His affection on you.

- Your father may have been an absentee dad. He could have died when you were a child (which was not his fault), or he could have abandoned you. He may have even been a "deadbeat dad" and avoided paying your mother the money needed to buy your food and clothes. But your heavenly Father is not that way. He is a generous Father, and He takes care of His own.

- Your father may have struggled with an addiction that changed his personality. He may have been highly unstable and unpredictable because of alcohol, drugs, or a traumatic emotional problem. Yet your heavenly Father is not that way. God is never unstable. He is always good, always kind, always just, and always loving. He says, "For I, the LORD, do not change" (Mal. 3:6). You will never have to worry about God's behavior becoming erratic, volatile, or inconsistent.

Let's Talk About It

1. Describe your home life as a child. If you had a father when you were growing up, tell us about him.
2. Look over the six dysfunctional fathers listed in the previous section. Does your father fit in any of these categories? (If not, share why you feel you had a good father.)
3. In what ways do you feel your father's behavior (either good or bad) has affected you today?
4. If your father failed you in some way, it is extremely important for you to forgive him from your heart. Meditate on the prayer below and say this from your heart.

Let's Pray About It

God, I acknowledge that I have unforgiveness in my heart toward my dad. Your Word says I cannot fully receive Your forgiveness for my own sins unless I am willing to forgive others. I choose to forgive my father for anything he did to hurt me. I release him into Your hands now. In Jesus's name, amen.

FILLING IN THE FATHER GAPS

No matter what kind of father you had—disciplinarian, passive, abusive, emotionally distant, absentee, addicted, or even if you had a really good father—you can be sure he was not perfect. No father can fully reflect the perfection of God's fatherly love. Therefore, all of us have deficiencies and wounds in our lives because of incomplete fathering.

Yet God does not leave us in this condition. He has made a way for us to be healed. This kind of healing does not happen overnight. In fact, discovering your heavenly Father's love is a life journey. But I recommend that you take the following steps:

1. **Make sure you have surrendered your life to Christ.**
   The path to healing can only begin after you have asked Jesus to live inside you. Only He can heal you. See the section titled "First Things First" at the end of the Introduction if you want to surrender your life to Christ for the first time.

2. **Identify your father wound.** An injury or sickness cannot be treated without a diagnosis. Through prayer and discussion with trusted friends, determine how you may have been wounded by your father's actions or inactions. Make sure you get rid of any resentment or bitterness toward him. (Make sure you forgive your mother as well. Sometimes mothers participate in similar behaviors or they support the father's bad habits.)

3. **Share your pain with a pastor or older Christian brother.** The Bible tells us to "bear one another's burdens" (Gal. 6:2). That means you must be transparent about your weakness and flaws in order to get help. If your dad abused you physically, be open about the pain. If you were constantly berated and criticized, talk about how this made you feel. If you need to cry about it, let the pain out. You are only hurting yourself if you bottle up your feelings.

4. **Find a role model, mentor, or spiritual father.** This can be an incredibly healing experience. Since I became a

Christian, God has put many godly men in my life. Some are my age, and some are much older. I relate to some of them as big brothers, others as coaches, and others as fathers in the faith. God has used each one of these men to fill in the gaps in my own spiritual life. They advise me, pray for me, encourage me, correct me, and—most of all—show unconditional love to me.

5. **Seek counseling.** If you lived in an extremely dysfunctional home, chances are you may need some professional counseling. Don't be ashamed of this. Some of the most successful people in the world have needed counseling to overcome serious emotional struggles. The important thing is that you talk with a counselor who bases his or her advice on biblical principles. To find the right counselor, consult with your pastor or call a local Christian counseling office.

6. **Saturate yourself in the love of God.** No person, not even the best pastor or spiritual father, can heal your heart as powerfully as your heavenly Father can. Often He will use people to do His healing work. But you must look to God to bring the ultimate healing you need. When you spend time reading His Word, look for signs of His love to you. Meditate on the goodness and mercy of God.

The main reason people fail in life is because they do not have a right concept of God. Make sure you have no distorted views of God in your mind. He is not an abuser. He will never neglect or forsake you. He loves you even when you make mistakes. Let God's Word renew your mind until you believe what the Scriptures say about Him. If you have believed lies about God, counteract those wrong ideas with the truth that is found in Scripture.

Most of all, remember that God has promised that He will be

"a father to the fatherless" (Ps. 68:5). That is not just a promise for orphans. Any man who has struggled because of a dysfunctional father can ask God to fill in the gaps and do what his earthy father failed to do.

It is a lie that you cannot be close to your father. If you are estranged from him, the Holy Spirit can bring reconciliation. And if your father is dead or is no longer accessible (or if you don't know where he is), it is still possible for you to have a close relationship with a spiritual father who can help to fill that void.

No matter what happened between you and your father on this earth, you can have a close and intimate relationship with your heavenly Father. Let God reach into every painful place in your heart. Let Him father you with His strong, nurturing love until you grow to be the man of God He intended you to be.

Let's Talk About It

1. Do you have a specific father wound? How would you identify it?
2. Can you identify an older man in your life who could be a mentor or spiritual father to you? Are you comfortable seeking a relationship like this? Why or why not?
3. Do you sometimes struggle to believe that God is as good as He says He is? Describe your doubts about God's character to the rest of the group.

In this country, you gotta make the money first. Then when you get the money, you get the power. Then when you get the power, then you get the women.[1]
—AL PACINO AS TONY MONTANA IN *SCARFACE*

I wasn't satisfied just to earn a good living. I was looking to make a statement.[2]
—DONALD TRUMP

Greed is good.[3]
—MICHAEL DOUGLAS AS GORDON GEKKO IN *WALL STREET*

I'm king of the world![4]
—JAMES CAMERON, UPON ACCEPTING AN OSCAR FOR HIS 1997 FILM *TITANIC*

Success is not measured by what a man accomplishes, but by the opposition he has encountered, and the courage with which he maintained the struggle against overwhelming odds.[5]
—CHARLES LINDBERGH

Do not love the world nor the things in the world. If anyone loves the world, the love of the Father is not in him. For all that is in the world, the lust of the flesh and the lust of the eyes and the boastful pride of life, is not from the Father but is from the world.
—1 JOHN 2:15–16

10 LIES

A REAL MAN IS DEFINED BY MATERIAL SUCCESS.

$\mathfrak{M}$Y WORLD WAS totally rocked in 2001 when I started doing ministry in developing countries. I thought I was going to these places to help needy people. What I soon discovered was that these "poor" people had a lot more to give me. This prompted me to do a major overhaul of my values and priorities. And each time I fly to another continent, I go through yet another process of reevaluation.

Back in 2009 I conducted a women's conference in Nairobi, Kenya. After I arrived, my host, a journalist named Gideon, mentioned that my "pastor friend from Malawi" was waiting to see me. I was surprised to hear this, since I wasn't aware that I had a pastor friend from Malawi! I've never been to that country, and I didn't remember talking to anyone from there.

"He says you've been e-mailing each other," Gideon told me. "And he arrived today to see you."

I vaguely remembered receiving a message a few months earlier from a man from somewhere in southern Africa. He asked if I would come to his country to speak at a conference, and I told him that I can't do events like that with people until I have met them and established a relationship of trust.

In a few hours I met this man, Pastor Peacepound. After a few minutes of small talk I learned that he had traveled on a crowded bus from Lilongwe, the capital of Malawi, to Nairobi. It was a four-day journey.

Four days on a bus? I was stunned. I've never met anyone in the United States who traveled that long to attend a Christian meeting. (We Americans simply aren't that spiritually desperate.) But this guy was so concerned about the way women are abused in his country—through domestic violence, molestation, and mutilation—that he made an astonishing sacrifice.

Then he stunned me again with a question. "You said you could not come to Malawi unless we met. Now that we have met, will you come?" he asked.

What was I supposed to say? I almost laughed out loud as I imagined a possible response. "Well, pastor, I'll have to pray about that," just didn't seem appropriate. How could I deny this man's petition when he had paid such an incredible price to visit me? What was there to pray about?

Pastor Peacepound's appeal was as sincere as it was humbling. Before the afternoon was over I had committed myself to coming to Lilongwe. I don't enjoy being away from my family that long. But when I consider the fact that my plane ride from the United States to Africa will take less time than Pastor Peacepound's famous bus ride, it puts things into perspective.

In my travels in the developing world I have met so many men like Pastor Peacepound. They know little of our Western comforts. They've never seen granite countertops, flat-screen TVs, iPods, or GPS systems. They've never shopped at a nice car dealership, a Sports Authority, a Best Buy store, a Bass Pro Shop, or even a Wal-Mart. They can't imagine needing garage door openers, leaf blowers, security systems, or the other suburban niceties we think are so crucial.

Gated communities, home theaters, or fast-food drive-throughs are unthinkable concepts to them.

These people often don't even have access to clean water or reliable electricity. They are just thankful to have enough rice and beans on the table. Yet as I have built friendships with Christian leaders in the developing world, God has totally messed with my suburban values.

My friend Raja, who rescues baby girls from trash cans in southeastern India after they have been thrown away, runs an orphanage for dozens of kids yet lives on a miniscule salary.

Lydia, a Christian lady I met in Kenya, runs a charitable school in Nairobi's largest slum and cares for numerous special-needs children—even though the school cannot cover her own living expenses.

Oto, a pastor I work with in Guatemala, feeds more than one hundred needy children every day—but he has no health insurance or retirement plan, and he has never been able to afford a vacation.

Biju, another friend from Mumbai, India, has the biggest smile of anyone I know. He and his wife, Secunda, feed hundreds of children who live on the edges of the world's largest garbage dump. Yet they live in a two-bedroom apartment with their two children in a high-rise building in one of the world's most crowded cities.

Moses, a pastor in Kampala, Uganda, has a two-hundred-member church that meets under a canopy in a slum area. His wife, mother, sister-in-law, and several children live in his tiny apartment. Yet he invited me and three friends to his home during my visit, and we enjoyed a dinner of chicken and rice. It was one of the most memorable meals I've ever eaten.

In these situations I looked at Raja, Lydia, Oto, Biju, and Moses and realized that they are rich in all the right ways.

These people do not have a lot of material comforts, but they do have shelter, food, close friendships, a close family, and—most of all—spiritual fulfillment. And they had overflowing joy and love. So what if they did not have the finest furniture, expensive appliances, or the latest entertainment systems? So what if they could not afford to see the latest 3-D Hollywood films or buy the newest iPhone?

So much of the world today is struggling while we Americans—even in times of economic recession—live at a level of unimaginable abundance. I'm not trying to lay a guilt trip on anyone. I don't think it is wrong to own a garage door opener or a nice car or house. But I think we should let reality sink in. The disparities we see between life in the sophisticated Western world and the third world should cause us to question our convoluted values. Maybe we really aren't as rich as we think we are.

RETHINKING YOUR PRIORITIES

I personally think we as men have been sold a bill of goods. Our culture tells us that we have to obtain certain material or physical achievements in order to have a life of true success. These requirements usually fall into one of six categories:

1. **Money.** According to worldly standards, a successful man must have at least a six-figure salary, leather upholstery in his BMW, a big house (and an extra vacation home), plenty of stock options, at least one luxury vacation a year, and a huge nest egg in his retirement account. And according to the gurus of high finance, it really doesn't make much difference where or how you make the money as long as you make lots of it and you have the right accountant to make you look good when the auditor shows up.

2. **Body.** Popular men's magazines tell us we have to have perfect, washboard abs, big pecs, and thick biceps to qualify for the "good life." One advertisement features a shirtless sixty-year-old man who has the chest and arms of a twenty-five-year-old athlete. The message: if you want to be successful, you have to defy the aging process.

3. **Sex.** Culture insists that a successful man should have sex on demand whenever he wants it, even if it means he must go outside the confines of his marriage to find the pleasure he needs. And today, because men are under such pressure to be sexual studs, even at age sixty-five, we have created a nation of Viagra addicts. Guys insist on maintaining the same rock-hard erections they had at age twenty-one, even if they have to use a drug to increase the blood flow.

4. **Power.** Many men believe the secret to true success is having lots of people following you—regardless of where you are going. This is why men spend thirty years in the same boring job; their goal in life is to obtain the oak-paneled corner office and a chance to sit at the end of the boardroom table. The deceptive allure of power even dupes Christian ministers; it's the only way to explain why flashy evangelists dressed in silk suits insist on being chauffeured in limousines to their "evangelistic" meetings.

5. **Fame.** We live in a nation that is drunk on celebrity. Many men want to be worshiped, whether they be politicians, rock singers, actors, businessmen, journalists, athletes, or just participants in a dumb reality TV show. People today even become famous just for being famous, even if they have never accomplished anything. The idea is that if your name becomes a household word or you can collect one hundred thousand followers on Twitter or Facebook, you are successful.

6. **Intellect.** Some guys are gifted athletes, while others have more brainpower. Both qualities are great assets—and yet we can end up idolizing either. Some guys in the academic world have been deceived into thinking that life revolves around their PhDs, research awards, or how

many books they've published. While their life's ambition may have begun with a desire to cure a disease or discover a solution to one of the world's problems, they fall into the pride trap and start thinking that the pursuit of knowledge alone makes them special.

We are all susceptible to this trap. God placed us in a material world full of shiny gold, glittering jewels, beautiful women, and huge tracts of real estate. Our sin nature blinds us to eternal realities, and we begin to look to *things* to satisfy us instead of *Him*. And the devil loves to dangle these temptations in front of us regularly so that we will bite the hook.

This was man's first mistake in the Garden of Eden. The sights and smells of the forbidden tree drew mankind away from intimacy with God. The lie that tempted Eve was an old one. Satan told her, "For God knows that on the day that you eat from [the tree] your eyes will be opened, and you will be like God, knowing good from evil" (Gen. 3:5). It was a tricky proposition: eat this and you won't need God; you can find success your own way.

Thousands of years later we are still making that deadly choice. We turn away from God to find our fulfillment through climbing the corporate ladder, amassing the biggest stock portfolio, having the best sex, and owning all the right toys. How can we be delivered from these wrong concepts of success? I recommend these three important steps.

1. CONSIDER THE BREVITY OF LIFE.

Funerals happen every day, but we only attend them occasionally. I believe we would all be better off if we went to more funerals—especially Christian funerals in which preachers read what the Bible says about heaven, hell, and eternity. Most men are in denial about what happens when they die.

David's son Solomon was one of the greatest kings who ever lived.

He had so much wealth that visiting dignitaries left his presence in awe. He had an expansive palace, a thousand concubines, a daily feast, innumerable vineyards and lush gardens, and the respect of a multitude. Yet after he collected all this fortune, he wrote in Ecclesiastes 2:10–11:

> All that my eyes desired I did not refuse them. I did not withhold my heart from any pleasure, for my heart was pleased because of all my labor and this was my reward for all my labor. Thus I considered all my activities which my hands had done and the labor which I had exerted, and behold all was vanity and striving after wind and there was no profit under the sun.

Solomon had more worldly success than any of us could ever hope to achieve, yet as he neared the end of his life, he concluded that he had been chasing after vain ambitions. He also wrote, "He who loves money will not be satisfied with money" (Eccles. 5:10). Even though he supposedly had it all, as his eyes grew dim he realized that all his material possessions and pleasures did not validate him or give true meaning to life.

I did some research on the world's five richest men. According to *Forbes* magazine's 2010 statistics, they are (1) Carlos Slim Helú, a Lebanese immigrant living in Mexico who amassed a $54 billion fortune in telecommunications; (2) Microsoft founder Bill Gates III, who is now worth $53 billion (and who stepped down from his company in 2008 to dedicate his life to philanthropy); (3) American investor Warren Buffett, who is worth $47 billion; (4) Mukesh Ambani, the son of an Indian tycoon (and dropout of Stanford University) who now owns an oil and gas conglomerate; and (5) Lakshmi Mittal, an Indian immigrant to England who owns the world's largest steel company.[6]

I am sure these men eat very well, drive some really nice cars, and have amazing art collections. They probably own much bigger houses than Solomon's palace. (Ambani, of India, actually lives in a twenty-seven-story home in Mumbai!) But what we must remember is that none of these men will take any of their money or their possessions into eternity. Even if they were buried with their cars and furniture like the pharaohs of ancient Egypt, none of their stuff would make it to the afterlife.

You've probably heard the familiar saying "There are no U-Hauls at the funeral parlor." When we stand before God we will not be evaluated by how we played the stock market or how many dinner guests we could fit in our mansions at one time. We won't be bringing our bankbooks into eternity. Solomon summarized this concept when he wrote, "As [man] had come naked from his mother's womb, so will he return as he came" (Eccles. 5:15).

Solomon also realized that man has been given a chance to understand eternal realities. He wrote in Ecclesiastes 3:11 (NLT, emphasis added):

> Yet God has made everything beautiful for its own time. *He has planted eternity in the human heart,* but even so, people cannot see the whole scope of God's work from beginning to end.

God has put a divine imprint on us. He made us for eternity. Deep down every man knows that his life is like a vanishing vapor (James 4:14) and that our time on Earth could end at any moment. That's why Satan uses material things to captivate us; the more we focus on the glimmering distractions of this world, the less we will think about our moral condition or how God will judge our lives after we die and meet Him.

Few of us spend much time planning our funerals or calculating when we might die. Recently I discovered a website called *The Death Clock* (www.death-clock.org) that actually calculates how much more time you have on Earth based on current life expectancy estimates. The user is asked to fill in his birth date, current health status, body mass index, and typical emotional mood. Then, after entering this data and clicking the "Submit" button, *voila!* It gives you an estimated date of your death and shows how many seconds you have left.

Sounds kind of morbid, but it might not be a bad idea for some people to visit this site regularly. Too many men are in complete denial about their mortality. Unless we are facing an illness, the loss of a relative, or some other type of tragedy, most of us don't think about the shortness of life. God sometimes allows these difficult interruptions in our lives to help adjust our temporal perspective.

Of course God wants us to enjoy the life He gives us on Earth. He wants to bless us in material ways. He gives us the power to make wealth so we can bless others (Deut. 8:18), He wants us to be physically fit so we can glorify Him in our bodies, He blesses us with sex in the context of marriage, and He gives us occupations so that we can honor Him through our work. But these gifts can become idols in our lives if we pursue them apart from God.

Personally, I have always placed a lot of importance on physical appearance, perhaps because I worried that I wasn't handsome enough to catch the attention of girls. When I was a teenager in the 1970s I idolized Burt Reynolds, the actor. He was the epitome of rugged masculinity with his athletic build, square jaw, and hairy chest. But as I watched Reynolds's career over the years (he is sixteen years older than I am), I realized that men don't stay virile and handsome forever. As he grew gray, my first gray hairs appeared. His chiseled physique didn't stay that way. Soon his face looked gaunt, reminding me that if I live long enough, I will look very, very old.

We are all going to shrivel up! And when we step into eternity, we will not take our money, our sports trophies, our accolades, our fan base, or our muscles. What we will take is our awakened conscience (or guilt), our compassion (or lack of it), our good deeds (or bad), our generosity (or stinginess), and our faith (or our doubts). The Bible says we will stand before the judgment seat of Christ to give an account for our deeds and to receive rewards for our faithfulness.

The apostle Paul warned the Corinthians to conduct their lives in light of this divine judgment. He said that the fire of heaven's holiness will test what we build in this life. He wrote in 1 Corinthians 3:12–15:

> Now if any man builds on the foundation with gold, silver, precious stones, wood, hay, straw, each man's work will become evident; for the day will show it because it is to be revealed with fire, and the fire itself will test the quality of each man's work. If any man's work which he has built on it remains, he will receive a reward. If any man's work is burned up, he will suffer loss; but he himself will be saved, yet so as through fire.

This is not simply an admonition to ministers about the way they build churches. It also applies to how you build your family, your career, your business, and your relationships—and how you make your fortune. If you build your life God's way, honoring His principles, you will have true success in the end. But if you build your life selfishly, using Satan's shoddy construction materials and following the world's building codes, you will prove yourself a failure even if you have enjoyed all the world's wealth and applause during your short time on Earth.

This is why Jesus Himself asked His disciples this question in Mark 8:36: "For what does it profit a man to gain the whole world, and forfeit his soul?" We should pray that the Holy Spirit would sear this haunting question into our minds each day as we grow closer and closer to eternity.

Let's Think About It

1. Some men think money is the requirement for success. Others place all the emphasis on fame. Think about the six areas of life we are tempted to idolize: money, body, sex, power, fame, and intellect. Which one of these do you tend to emphasize the most? Why?
2. Have you ever faced the death of a friend or relative? Did this experience change the way you view your own life? In what way?
3. If success is not about money, power, or fame, what do you think are the most important values? What makes a man truly successful?

2. FIND GODLY ROLE MODELS.

I can't reveal my Pakistani friend's name, so I will just call him Saleem. I met this young church leader during a missions conference in Pennsylvania in 2009. The same day we met, Islamic radicals were burning Christian houses to the ground in an area not far from Saleem's city. Twenty believers were killed when the Taliban attacked the peaceful settlement.

One of Saleem's friends was severely wounded in the attack. This kind of violence happens often in Pakistan, where so-called blasphemy laws make it a capital offense to tear a page of the Islamic holy book or to insult the name of Muhammad.

Saleem lifted up his sleeve and showed me two scars near his elbow and wrist. They mark where a bullet passed from one end of his arm to the other when Islamic militants shot him in the city of Lahore in 2005. If you take a close look at Saleem's scalp, under his thick black hair you will find many scars from where he was beaten on the head with sticks.

"Many members of my church have been put in jail because of

'blasphemy' laws," Saleem said—noting that all such charges against his congregation were false. Saleem receives untraceable text messages almost every day from Taliban members threatening to kill him.

Islamic militants are upset because Christianity is growing more rapidly in Pakistan than anyone in government will admit. Official statistics say Pakistan is 2 percent Christian. Saleem claims the figure is much higher. He says many former Muslims won't state their religion in surveys because they fear reprisals from radical Islamists—and because Christians are denied jobs and forced to live in ghettos.

Although Saleem leads a network of nine hundred house churches in his city (with an average membership of two hundred each), he is not a wealthy man. He and his wife and son share a small house with six other family members. There are bullet holes in their front gate. They keep a water buffalo nearby and sell its milk to make extra money.

Miracles have followed this young pastor, who began directing his church network in 1997. In May 2008, a Muslim man brought his dead six-year-old son to an evangelistic meeting. Said Saleem, "I saw the fire of God on that child, and he was revived. It was the presence of God. It wasn't me. The doctor stood in the meeting and gave a report. He said the child had been dead."

In most of Saleem's outdoor meetings, up to 80 percent of the audience is Muslim. Huge numbers of them are converted to Christ when they see displays of God's miracle power. "We have seen blind eyes opened, the paralyzed walk, deaf ears opened," he told me. "We see people get out of wheelchairs. We see many miracles performed in Jesus's name."

It is one thing to read about persecuted Christians like Saleem. It was quite another experience to eat several meals with this brother, listen to him pray in his native Urdu language, and look at the brand marks on his body. Two days with Saleem forced me to do a reality check.

I realized at the time that I had been complaining in my heart about trivial things—the price of gasoline, the sour economy, and the slowness of some Internet connections. Suddenly I felt ridiculous. I repented for my ungrateful attitude. And then I thanked God for a new role model who was almost young enough to be my son.

I have met many other "living martyrs" like Saleem in the past ten years.

Zhang Rongliang is one of the most prominent leaders of China's underground house church movement. About four years after I met him in a city in southeastern China, he was sentenced to seven and a half years in prison after being charged with illegal border crossing and other crimes.

Affectionately known as "Brother Z," Zhang had already spent twelve years in prison since he was secretly baptized in 1969. He was often tortured during those years. The first thing that struck me when I met him was that he did not look like the leader of ten million Christians. Often wearing unkempt navy trousers and a wrinkled blue shirt, his black hair tousled, he easily blends into the crowd when mingling among the millions in China's Henan province.

But he is no ordinary peasant from Henan. This simple man—who prefers to sit on the floor when meeting with his team—is an apostle who has planted thousands of churches since the early 1970s. Foreign missionaries and Chinese church workers alike consider him the most influential leader in the church in China.

Like a New Testament apostle, Zhang bears the brand marks of suffering. He has endured beatings with iron rods and bayonets. He was even shocked with an electric cattle prod.

Converted to Christ in 1963 at age thirteen, Zhang attended covert house churches in rural areas of Henan—where Mao Tse-Tung's dreaded Public Security Bureau (PSB) officials were on the lookout for religious "counterrevolutionaries." In 1974, PSB officers handcuffed him and beat him with sticks to force him to reveal information about his Christian activities. His refusal to deny his faith or betray his colleagues landed him in the Xi Hua labor camp for seven years.

Yet like the apostle Paul, Zhang's faith thrived even while he was imprisoned. After Zhang was released from Xi Hua in 1980, he founded the Chinese for Christ movement—a vast network of churches that had grown to an estimated ten million members by the year 2001. "It is impossible to know the accurate number," Zhang told me. "It's like the census of China. You can never be sure. Even while we are talking here, we are starting churches. The work of God's kingdom is so fast."

Men like Brother Z in China and "Saleem" in Pakistan have provided me a whole new perspective on success. Neither of these men will achieve anything close to the materialistic American dream, but they are my heroes. They've shown me what is most important in life: bravery, dauntless faith, fierce love for God, and compassion for people. These Christians from the third world remind me of the Old Testament heroes of faith described in the Book of Hebrews. It is said of them:

> They were stoned, they were sawn in two, they were tempted, they were put to death with the sword; they went about in sheepskins, in goatskins, being destitute, afflicted, ill-treated (men of whom the world was not worthy), wandering in deserts and mountains and caves and holes in the ground.
>
> —HEBREWS 11:37–38

The normal definition of *success* does not usually include affliction, poverty, or martyrdom. But the Bible usually contradicts our worldly standards. If you have become safe and comfortable in your suburban American bubble, I encourage you to find some new role models. They don't have to be from China or Pakistan; you may need to spend time with an immigrant pastor in your city or with the man in your church who has been visiting prisoners every week for twenty years. I guarantee that if you hang around with men like these, their priorities will become yours.

3. FIND YOUR VALIDATION FROM GOD ALONE.

Because of our misplaced cultural values, many men today are addicted to success. Our lives totally revolve around our performance, and we simply cannot allow ourselves to fail. This is called "performance orientation." A man who is bent in this direction bases his personal worth not on *who he is* but on *what he does.*

Performance orientation can lead to all kinds of dysfunction. It drives men to compete with each other in business, producing a cutthroat atmosphere in the workplace instead of helpful camaraderie. It can push athletes to use steroids or other illegal drugs. The all-consuming desire to win at all costs is what leads many professional men into ethical compromise or even criminal activity.

Performance orientation can also be deadly. In some Asian countries, men who are fired from their jobs sometimes commit suicide because they cannot bear to tell their families they failed.

We sometimes call these men overachievers, and we assume that it is normal behavior for a CEO or entrepreneur. There certainly is nothing wrong with having a drive to succeed in business. But there is a difference between having a drive and being driven.

Men who are driven—whether they are corporate executives, politicians, entertainers, or ministers—usually end up hurting people in their aggressive pursuit of personal success. That's because their drive is a selfish one: they are desperately trying to prove their unique value to everyone around them. In other words, success is all about them.

Driven men usually develop this tendency because they never felt they could please their own fathers. Out of frustration and a sense of self-doubt, they overcompensate. They say to themselves, "OK, I am going to show my dad that I am something. I'll prove to him and everybody else that I am not the failure he told me I was." And so the painful process begins. This tormented overachiever will probably make his way to the top of the corporate ladder, but not without first ruining the lives of his coworkers and his own family.

The solution for performance orientation lies in a simple revelation, but it is not easy to grasp if you have been conditioned as an overachiever. God wants us to understand that His love is not based on our behavior or whether we carried out every assignment perfectly. His love is free, unmerited, and undeserved.

The best way to explain God's love for us is to look at Jesus on the day of His baptism in the River Jordan. The Bible tells us that after Jesus came up from the water, the heavens opened, the Holy Spirit descended like a dove from heaven, and the Father's voice declared, "This is My beloved Son, in whom I am well-pleased" (Matt. 3:17).

We have to remember that this remarkable scene occurred before Jesus had performed any miracles. He had not healed any sick people, preached any sermons, fed any multitudes, or cast out any demons. And He certainly had not carried His cross or paid for the sins of the world. Yet God pronounced this amazing blessing over His Son in front of everyone!

And so it is with us. Your heavenly Father loves you; He is proud of you and He calls you "Daddy's boy." He does not base His approval of you on anything you have done or haven't done. It is strictly because of His relationship with you. And your Father wants you to become so secure in that intimate relationship that you derive your worth and value not from your actions but from His fatherhood.

Notice that right after Jesus was baptized, the devil came to Him and tempted Him in the wilderness. Satan's first words in that scene are highly suspicious. He tells Jesus, *"If you are the Son of God,* command that these stones become bread" (Matt. 4:3, emphasis added). Satan says it again in verse 6: *"If you are the Son of God,* throw Yourself down."

This is exactly what the devil does in our lives. He tries to tempt us to doubt our sonship. He knows that if we begin to question our relationship with God, we will eventually seek security in other things.

Are you a son? Are you secure in the fact that God loves you no matter what mistakes you have made in life? Do you believe He approves of you without any reservations? Or do you imagine that God is shaking His head in disgust when you approach Him?

When the Father spoke His blessing over Jesus at His baptism, God did not whisper His blessing or wait until Jesus was alone to offer it. This was not a half-hearted display of approval. God shouted His commendation over the crowd for all to hear. And it is important to note that the tense of the Greek verb in the phrase "I am well-pleased" is a timeless and emphatic one. It means that God had always been pleased with Jesus and always would be.[7]

It is the same with you, my brother. If you are a believer in Christ and Jesus lives in you, then you have access to the same wholehearted approval from your heavenly Father that He gave the Son. God is overjoyed with you. You are His boy. You don't have to work for His blessing or jump through hoops to win His affection. You don't have to do anything to overcompensate for your mistakes or shortcomings. You don't have anything to prove. Just relax and enjoy His love. It is yours simply because you are His beloved son—in whom the Father is well pleased.

Let's Talk About It

1. Whom do you look up to as models of success? Why?
2. In what ways do persecuted Christians in other countries challenge our American views of success?
3. Many men are on a constant search for approval because they did not get it from their own fathers. Why is this kind of performance orientation so unhealthy?
4. Be honest: do you believe God loves you just as you are, or are you striving to win His approval, as well as the approval of others?

Let's Pray About It

Father, I know I cannot buy Your love or work to earn it. Please set me free from all striving for approval. Help me to understand that I don't have to perform to win Your affection. Give me a revelation of Your unconditional love. In Jesus's name, amen.

Woman in her greatest perfection was made to serve and obey man.[1]
—JOHN KNOX, SCOTTISH REFORMER

Let us set our women folk on the road to good-ness by teaching them...to display...submissiveness, to observe in silence. Every woman should be overwhelmed with shame at the thought that she is a woman.[2]
—ST. CLEMENT OF ALEXANDRIA

Sensible and responsible women do not want to vote. The relative positions to be assumed by man and woman in the working out of our civilization were assigned long ago by a higher intelligence than ours.[3]
—GROVER CLEVELAND, AMERICAN PRESIDENT

Nature intended women to be our slaves. They are our property.[4]
—NAPOLEON BONAPARTE

When a woman becomes a scholar there is usually something wrong with her sexual organs.[5]
—FRIEDRICH NIETZSCHE, GERMAN PHILOSOPHER

Women should be obscene and not heard.[6]
—GROUCHO MARX, COMEDIAN

The obvious and fair solution to the housework problem is to let men do the housework for, say, the next six thousand years, to even things up. The trouble is that over the years, men have developed an inflated notion of everything they do, so that before long they would turn housework into just as much a charade as business is now. They would hire secretaries and buy computers and fly off to house-work conferences in Bermuda, but they'd never clean anything.[7]
—DAVE BARRY, COLUMNIST

10 𝔏𝔦𝔢𝔰

𝔏𝔦𝔢 #4

A MAN IS THE ULTIMATE "BOSS" OF HIS FAMILY.

I N THE 1975 science-fiction movie *The Stepford Wives*, a young couple named Walter and Joanna Eberhart move from New York City to Stepford, a quiet, upscale suburb in Connecticut.[8] They want to get away from the fast pace of the city, but they get more than they bargained for when Walter begins to attend a men-only club called the Stepford Men's Association.

Joanna doesn't like the secrecy of the organization, and she becomes more troubled by the fact that all the women she meets in Stepford are extremely compliant. All the wives talk about is their domestic duties and their children's activities. None of the women seem to have any personal goals or interests. They act like doormats.

Things become stranger when Joanna and her feisty, freethinking friend Bobbie begin to investigate the odd behavior of the women. Suddenly, Bobbie's personality changes, and she too becomes rigidly compliant and overly submissive—as if she has been brainwashed.

As the film moves toward its bizarre climax, Joanna breaks into a room in the men's club and makes a horrifying discovery. She finds a mechanical mannequin that looks exactly like her, only its hollow, lifeless eyes are dilated so much that they are totally black. She realizes that the sinister-looking replica has been prepared to replace her.

As it turns out, the men of Stepford didn't really want their wives to be their partners. They wanted robots they could control.

Some critics dismissed *The Stepford Wives* back in the 1970s as a goofy diatribe against feminism. But we could actually learn a few lessons from it. There are Christian men today who act as though they prefer robotic wives. I talk to men like this regularly.

During a ministry trip to Hungary in 2009, I heard a painfully familiar story. Through a translator, a tearful young woman living near Budapest explained that her Christian husband was angrily demanding her absolute submission. This included, among other things, that she clean their house according to his strict standards and that she engage in sexual acts with him that made her feel uncomfortable and dirty.

This lady was not demanding her rights or trying to be disrespectful. She was a godly, humble woman who obviously wanted to please the Lord. But she had been beaten to a pulp emotionally, and she was receiving little help from her pastor—who was either unwilling or unprepared to confront wife abuse.

I've heard so many sickening versions of this scenario. When I visited Kenya, several women told me their AIDS-infected husbands often raped them—and then their pastors told them they must submit to this treatment. In some parts of India even some pastors believe it is acceptable to beat their wives if they argue with them or show any form of disrespect. And in some conservative churches in the United States women are told that obedience to God is measured by their wifely submission—even if their husbands are addicted to alcohol or pornography, or if they are involved in adulterous affairs.

This distortion of biblical teaching has plunged countless Christian women into depression and emotional trauma. I'm not sure which is worse: the harsh words they hear from their husbands or the perverse way the Bible is wielded as a leather belt to justify a form of domestic slavery.

Even godly men who would never think of hurting their wives physically have unknowingly subjected them to painful emotional abuse by demanding total obedience in the name of "biblical submission." But is their version of submission really biblical? I've asked men to tell me what they think submission in marriage really means, and they often refer to a vague concept of "male headship," which they base on Ephesians 5:23. This verse says: "For the husband is the head of the wife, as Christ also is head of the church, He Himself being the Savior of the body."

What is male headship? I get a wide variety of answers when I ask men to explain it. Here are some of their responses:

- Being the "male head" means that when my wife and I disagree, I break the tie.
- Being the head of my home means I am the boss. The buck stops with me, and I make all the rules.
- Being the head of my home means I have a priestly responsibility to pray for my wife and children. God holds me responsible for their spiritual well-being.
- Being the head of my home means I have a responsibility to lead my wife and children in spiritual things like prayer, devotions, and Bible study.
- Being the head of my home means that when I felt my wife and I should adopt a child and she didn't want to, I made an "executive decision," and we went through with the adoption. As the husband, I should make those hard choices.
- Being the head of my house means that when we go on vacation, I plan the schedule.

I even know a guy who insists that he should always drive when he and his wife are traveling in their car together. He feels that if he allows his wife to drive him, he abdicates his headship role! And some Christian fundamentalists have rigidly taught that since a man is the head of his home, he should always be in the dominant position (on top) during sexual intercourse. Christian missionaries in some foreign countries actually promoted this idea in the last century, and it provided the origin of the phrase *missionary position*. (Other sex positions, such as woman-on-top, were rejected as pagan—even though the Bible never advocates any specific style of sexual intercourse.)

There are Christians who believe that the concept of headship denotes some type of dictatorial control in marriage. They cite the Ephesians 5:23 verse, as well as another verse in 1 Corinthians 11:3:

> But I want you to understand that Christ is the head of every man, and the man is the head of a woman, and God is the head of Christ.

The casual reader might assume from reading this passage that God set up marriage as a hierarchy. Yet the Greek word used to denote "head" in both of these passages is *kephale*, a word that does not have anything to do with heavy-handed authority. If Paul had meant to imply autocratic subservience, he would have used a more common word, *archon*. The word *kephale* can either mean "source" (as in the source of a river) or "one who leads into battle" (as a forerunner). Neither original definition of this word gives room for control, abuse, or dictatorial rule.

Headship, in its essence, is not about "who's the boss." It is really about "who's the source." The husband is the "source" of the wife because the first woman originated from the first man, and as a result she was intimately connected to him in a mystical union that is unlike any other human relationship.

When Eve was taken from Adam's side and then presented to

him, he recited what appears to be a poem about this beautiful new creation. He says in Genesis 2:23:

> This is now bone of my bones, and flesh of my flesh; she shall be called Woman, because she was taken out of Man.

Many Bibles set off this passage as poetry, but some scholars believe it is actually a song. Consider the possibility that the first song in the Bible was a love song from a husband to his wife! There was serious romance in the Garden of Eden, and the first man had a serious case of lovesickness. Also notice that what he celebrates in his anthem is the fact that the woman came from him. Adam finds it special that this mesmerizingly beautiful creature called "woman" found her source in the man's rib.

The fact that he is her "head," or her "source," makes his relationship with her romantic and unique as well as deeply spiritual. It unites them as partners forever. They share a holy, mystical connection that is even more enhanced when they have sexual intercourse. But their bond transcends sex; it is a spiritual union that was created and blessed by God Himself.

This is the real power of headship. It is all about connection, bonding, and mutuality. When a man sees himself as the head of his wife, it reminds him that she is his equal, that she came from him, and that they share a special, covenantal connection that is designed to last for life. When a woman sees her husband as her head, she delights in his protection and prizes the encouragement and affection that flows from his river of love. And she acknowledges that this connection is a lifelong bond. Marriage, as it was intended in the beginning, is an opportunity for a male and a female to share the amazing depths of God's love over their entire lifetime.

Headship also reminds us that the bond between a husband and a wife is more important than any other human connection. In fact, when God gave Eve to Adam, He told him that he would have to sever his primary connection to his parents. God said in Genesis 2:24:

> For this reason a man shall leave his father and his mother,
> and be joined to his wife.

This is also true for a woman. When she is joined to her husband in marriage, she no longer looks to her parents as her primary source. God creates a new family with each matrimonial bond. In ancient times, fathers sometimes would claim ownership over their daughters' husbands or their possessions (as Laban attempted to do when Jacob fled with Rachael and Leah in Genesis 31:22–23). Yet God overrules this arrangement. The father is not the head of the married daughter, and in-laws do not have rights to stake their claim on a newlywed couple.

Never, ever was headship meant to be about power, position, or authority. Never was the man to stand between his wife and her relationship with God, nor was he to stand over her like some kind of God-appointed policeman. The original plan has always been that the husband and wife would walk in divine unity as one and together would place the Lord at the center of their covenant.

Let's Talk About It

1. Ephesians 5:23 and 1 Corinthians 11:3 both refer to the husband as the "head" of the wife. What do you think this means?

2. We talked about two Greek words—*archon*, which means "boss," and *kephale*, which can mean "leader" or "source." In what ways is a husband the "source" of his wife?

3. The first man, Adam, actually found it exciting that his wife had been taken out of his side. He saw his wife as an equal partner. Do you view your wife this way, or do you feel she is just supposed to obey you and go along with whatever you say?

4. In what ways could you improve the level of intimacy in your marriage?

A CHRISTLIKE VIEW OF LEADERSHIP

So, the question remains: "Who's the boss?" Is the husband the ultimate "boss" in his marriage?

I don't look at marriage that way. I view my wife, Deborah, as an equal partner. We are a team. When we were married on April 28, 1984, the minister declared this over us by reading these solemn words from Genesis 2:24: "They shall become one flesh." We asked the Lord to come into our relationship and be the ultimate boss!

My wife and I share everything. We enjoy a physical, emotional, and spiritual unity. Of course we have disagreements, but I don't slam my fist on the table and shout, "I am the head of this home, and you must do as I command!" That would be a dictatorship, not a marriage. That is not what my wife signed up for when she stood at the altar, and that is not how I promised to treat her.

If Deborah and I don't reach an agreement, we determine to pray together until we have consensus. We defer to one another and prefer one another. I don't just wait around until she agrees with my opinion; sometimes I change my view and go with what she feels is right. I am not afraid to admit that I am wrong. I don't want my wife to agree with me just because I am "the man in charge"; I want us both to agree with God! Men who insist on being right all the time are insecure and arrogant.

There is no scripture in the Bible that gives a husband autocratic control of his marriage or that enthrones him in some kind of elevated position of superiority. In fact, Jesus declared that in the kingdom of God, heavy-handed control has been replaced in the new covenant by a concept of servant leadership that is marked by humility. Jesus said in Matthew 20:25–28:

But Jesus called them to Himself and said, "You know that the rulers of the Gentiles lord it over them, and their great men exercise authority over them. It is not this way among you, but whoever wishes to become great among you shall be your servant, and whoever wishes to be first among you shall be your slave; just as the Son of Man did not come to be served, but to serve, and to give His life a ransom for many."

Based on this view of Christian leadership, a man who is bossing his wife around in a rigid, authoritarian manner has adopted a pagan style of governing. A man who views himself as the affectionate, loving "head" of his wife would never treat her harshly, deny her full personhood, or abuse her in any way. And he is secure enough in his manhood to admit when he's wrong.

God's design for marriage is not a hierarchy but a loving, nurturing, equal partnership that is characterized by physical intimacy, spiritual oneness, and mutual submission. Yet it does not come easy for us guys. We are bent by sin in the direction of domination, control, and abuse. Pride comes naturally for us. But if we invite Christ to change our hearts, then we can fully expect that He will change the way we treat our wives.

Are you willing to allow Jesus Christ to change you? Whenever I speak to men about their marriages, I always challenge them to become the "head" of their wives in three radical ways.

1. You must first love your wife as an equal.

One of the main reasons there is so much tension in Christian marriages (and why the divorce rate is so high among churchgoers) is false or unbalanced teaching about submission. If you view your wife as a child or as an unequal partner who has no right to her own opinion, then you are inviting serious problems into your relationship.

When Paul wrote his New Testament epistles, husbands basically owned their wives. Women had no civil rights, and they were typically dragged around like domesticated animals. They were rarely given any educational opportunities and in most cases were illiterate; they were viewed as servants, sex objects, and baby-making machines. (Not to mention the fact that many men in biblical times had multiple wives, and women are always viewed as inferior in polygamous cultures.)

Yet Paul dramatically contradicted this pagan view of women and announced that the gospel had brought them a new dignity. He told the men in the Ephesian church, "So husbands ought to love their own wives as their own bodies" (Eph. 5:28). He also said to husbands in the same chapter, "Each individual among you also is to love his own wife even as himself" (v. 33).

This was a radical message in Paul's day. Greeks certainly did not believe women deserved love or dignity. Yet this is the Christian way, and it is the attitude Christ modeled in all His dealings with women during His earthly ministry. The apostle Peter continued this theme in his first epistle when he warned men that God would not answer their prayers if they embraced a low opinion of their wives. He wrote in 1 Peter 3:7:

> You husbands in the same way, live with your wives in an understanding way, as with someone weaker, since she is a woman; and show her honor as a fellow heir of the grace of life, so that your prayers will not be hindered.

Peter does not negate the fact that there are differences between men and women. God certainly wants men to be masculine and women to be feminine. Gender differences are part of the creation order, and it is wrong for anyone to deny that or try to change it.

But man's inherent masculine characteristics (such as physical strength) are never to be used to dominate his wife. On the contrary, God says He will oppose a man if he mistreats his wife, views her as an inferior, or throws his weight around in a chauvinistic way. No matter how strong a man is, he does not want God opposing him!

Peter was teaching us here that in the kingdom of heaven, the strong must learn to be meek. Our strength must be tempered. According to this passage, men who honor their wives as equal partners and esteem them as "fellow heirs" of God's grace will enjoy true power and authority. Meanwhile those who abuse their fleshly power by acting like the "boss" will actually risk losing that authority.

2. Second, you must learn to serve your wife.

When I started traveling to Latin America to preach, I noticed that when we had meetings of pastors they rarely brought their wives. Finally I asked why, and one brother gave an honest answer: "They need to stay home so they can cook."

In so many developing cultures, women practically live in the kitchen. This is their world. Their day begins in the kitchen with cooking breakfast, and by the time they wash the morning dishes and do the day's laundry, it is time to fix another meal. Sometimes preparing food also involves fetching water from a well, killing a chicken, walking to the market more than once a day, peeling vegetables, carrying firewood, and grinding meal.

In the macho culture of Latin America you will rarely find a man in the kitchen. He might work hard harvesting watermelons, repairing roads, or driving trucks, but only a secure man cooks. It is more likely that you will find him relaxing in his hammock on the porch while his wife is cooking tortillas in a hot kitchen. This is the ironclad tradition of the culture.

So you can imagine what kinds of reactions I get when I suggest to these *hombres duros* ("tough guys") that they should show Christ's love to their wives by serving them in the kitchen. Usually the men either laugh nervously or look at me with blank stares. Serving their wives is a foreign concept. In many households in countries such as Mexico, Guatemala, or Ecuador, wives are simply maids—only they are not paid.

We also find this chauvinistic attitude in more prosperous Western countries where women have equal opportunities in the workplace and access to advanced educational degrees. In some American households where both husband and wife work full-time jobs, the husband expects the wife to do all the cooking, laundry, and housework since that is "woman's work." This kind of attitude is degrading to a woman. It tells her she is inferior. If we want to model Christ in our homes, we must be willing to challenge cultural traditions, even if they have been passed down in our own families.

When a man and woman marry, they must access their work schedules and lovingly divide up the chores so there is a fair division of labor. If the family setup is more traditional, with the man working a full-time job and the woman staying home with small children, then it is totally fair for the woman to take on more of the domestic responsibilities since her husband will not have time for those. But if both spouses work, the husband and wife need to equally share those duties. There is no scripture in the Bible that says women must do all the cooking or childcare.

My wife and I had a more traditional setup when our four children were young. I went to work each day and left Deborah to care for our girls, and this arrangement worked best for us. But sometimes when I would come home from work, and my daughters would run to the door to greet me, I could see the fatigue in my wife's face. As much as she loved being a stay-at-home mom, she sometimes felt overwhelmed. There was always a diaper to be changed, a nose to be wiped, a spill to clean up, or an argument to arbitrate. A mother's work is truly never done.

So there were times when I would tell my wife to take a Saturday off. I encouraged her to go for coffee with a friend or just go shopping. I knew she needed some breathing room so she would not suffocate under all these motherly pressures. She would leave the house, and I would do my best to change the diapers, fix the sandwiches, clean up the spills, and take the girls somewhere for fun.

I can assure you that when those "daddy days" came to an end,

I was more than exhausted. Serving my wife in that way helped me understand the fatigued look I had seen in her face so many times. And this helped me develop a deeper appreciation for all my wife did to care for our family.

I believe this is the "Jesus way" to love your wife. You must serve her! This is what Paul meant when he told husbands to love their wives "as Christ loved the church." (See Ephesians 5:25–26.) In that passage, Paul refers to cleansing the wife "by the washing of water of the word." This is a reference to the day when Jesus washed the feet of His disciples at the Passover meal before His crucifixion.

Jesus exemplified servant leadership to His followers by washing their feet. In biblical times, foot washing was a task only carried out by the lowest rank of servants. No macho guy in ancient Israel would ever stoop so low as to touch a dirty sandal. Yet what did Jesus do? He took off His robe, put on the towel of a household slave, and showed His disciples true, humble leadership.

As husbands we must be willing to do the same at home. We must be willing to get our hands dirty doing things that don't come naturally to us. That might mean spreading peanut butter on bread, sticking your hands in soapy dishwater, or cleaning spilled food off of a high chair. Ask yourself, What would Jesus do? If He would serve your wife, then you should follow Him instead of acting like a macho man who thinks he is too tough to do housework.

3. You must empower your wife.

In 2006 I spoke at a pastors' conference in the Punjab region of northern India. The pastors were urged to bring their wives to the conference, but this was uncomfortable for them because they had never included their wives in any aspect of church work. Most of the women, in fact, said this was the first time they had ever been invited to any type of conference. One of the women told me, "Usually we just feel like we are our husband's luggage."

During that conference I did a special meeting just for the ladies, and I brought some women from the United States who could minister to them through preaching and prayer. By the end of that session the women were glowing with excitement. Many of them had experienced the infilling of the Holy Spirit for the first time; others were encouraged to use their spiritual gifts; others were freed from depression or other emotional problems.

As I looked out over the audience of women, the kaleidoscope of color struck me. Indian women wear flowing robes called *saris.* The varied fabrics in the church that day ranged from turquoise to sky blue to canary yellow to pink to lavender. While the women were worshiping I could sense the Lord's delight as He enjoyed this colorful display. The different hues reminded me of the varied spiritual gifts that God had given these precious women—gifts that they never even realized they had.

It also made me sad to realize that these women had been in church for many years and were married to pastors, yet no one had encouraged them to step out in ministry. Some of them had gifts of leadership and teaching. Others were graced by God to work with children or to lead prayer groups. Many were called to disciple women. But never until that day had anyone even noticed them. They were invisible. And their husbands were blind to their potential.

What about your wife? Do you know what her spiritual gifts are? Have you encouraged those gifts or challenged her to step into her full potential? Or have you felt threatened by your wife because you worried that she would be perceived as more spiritual than you?

In many churches today there is an unwritten rule that men must always lead the way. Women who have leadership gifts are viewed with suspicion, and they are urged to put their spiritual ambitions on a shelf. The underlying assumption is that since God created man first and made him "head of the woman," man must always be dominant in spiritual things.

That may sound like a convincing theory, but it has no scriptural basis. God doesn't always go to a man first when He wants to start something. There are plenty of examples in the Bible when God called on women to accomplish His plans. In fact, God's ultimate plan for the redemption of the world was revealed to a young girl, Mary, who was chosen to bear the Savior. God did not send the annunciation angel to Joseph first to get his permission, nor did God seek Mary's father's approval first.

Joseph probably would have broken his betrothal to Mary if God had not later given him detailed instructions in a dream. The Bible says that Joseph planned to send Mary away secretly, presumably to end the engagement and to protect her from public punishment for being pregnant outside of wedlock. Notice what the angel said to Joseph in Matthew 1:20:

> But when he had considered this, behold, an angel of the Lord appeared to him in a dream, saying, "Joseph, son of David, do not be afraid to take Mary as your wife; for the Child who has been conceived in her is of the Holy Spirit."

After receiving these instructions, Joseph became Mary's protector. He recognized there was something holy growing inside her. He marveled at the work of God in her. He protected her from insults and shame during the pregnancy and helped her give birth to the baby Jesus in Bethlehem. When Herod's murderous plot became known, Joseph took Mary and the child to Egypt. He did everything in his power to shield Mary and her offspring from danger.

Joseph now shines as a model husband to all of us. We should take our cues from him. Your wife is not carrying the infant Messiah inside her, but if she is a Christian, she does carry the call of God. She has gifts and talents that have been entrusted to her. Yet those spiritual graces need to be nurtured, blessed, and encouraged. All women have the potential to accomplish something great for God, but often they never achieve this because their husbands either ignore their gifts out of ignorance or they crush them with criticism and negativity.

Which kind of man are you? The kind who keeps his wife quiet and marginalized, afraid that she might outshine him in some way? Or are you willing for your wife to be successful? A humble, secure man will praise his wife's character, validate her talents, help fund her education, give her opportunities, and congratulate her successes. A woman who is empowered in that way by a loving husband will end up making a mark in history.

Let's Talk About It

1. What is the most Christlike way for a husband and wife to resolve a disagreement?
2. Jesus modeled a new kind of leadership by washing the feet of His disciples. How can you model servant leadership in your home? (And if you are not married, how do you plan to do this in your marriage?)
3. Do you feel that you and your wife have fairly divided the workload in your home? Is there any room for improvement?
4. Make a list of your wife's talents and spiritual gifts. How can you encourage her to develop her potential?

Let's Pray About It

Father, help me to view my wife as a valued equal partner. I recognize that You have deposited something holy in my wife. Just as Mary carried the Christ child, I know my wife carries a ministry from God. Help me to protect and nurture all that You have placed inside her. Help me to speak positive words of life to her rather than criticism. Amen.

*I always say now that I'm in my blonde years. Because since the
end of my marriage, all of my girlfriends have been blonde.*[1]
—HUGH HEFNER, PUBLISHER OF *PLAYBOY* MAGAZINE

---

*I do not think that there are any men who
are faithful to their wives.*[2]
—JACQUELINE KENNEDY ONASSIS

---

*When a man of forty falls in love with a girl of twenty,
it isn't her youth he is seeking but his own.*[3]
—LENORE COFFEE

Boys will be boys, and so will a lot of middle-aged men.[4]
—KIN HUBBARD

---

10 LIES

SEX IS PRIMARILY FOR THE MAN'S ENJOYMENT, NOT THE WOMAN'S.

IN THE 2008 film *Slumdog Millionaire*, two desperately poor brothers in India, Jamal and Salim, befriend a poor orphaned girl named Latika.[5] The boys' mother has just been killed in a religious riot between Hindus and Muslims. All three children are then captured by crime bosses and forced to work as beggars on the streets of Mumbai, so they decide to escape. The boys are able to jump on a moving train, but Latika cannot run as fast, and she ends up remaining in captivity with her cruel owners. At that point Jamal vows to find his friend no matter what it takes.

A few years later, after Jamal becomes a teenager, he learns from one of his blind orphan friends that Latika has been forced to work as a prostitute in Mumbai's infamous red-light district. He and Salim go to this place, which is called Kamathipura. They are horrified to find hundreds of young women and girls who provide sex to male customers, all for the profit of their owner pimps. Each girl works in a filthy stall that is only a few feet wide. The boys are able to rescue Latika just before a middle-aged man steals her virginity.

I wish I could say this is only a scene from a movie, but Kamathipura is a real place. Back in the 1990s there were more than fifty thousand women and girls working in this brothel district. Some of them had been brought there from Nepal and other countries and were drugged and beaten into submission until they agreed to work for their bosses.

During a visit to Mumbai in 2009 I met with Biju Thampy, an Indian missionary who has planted a church and feeding center near the world's largest garbage dump. Biju told me that he once led a young prostitute to Jesus Christ while he was preaching the gospel near Kamathipura. The girl had contracted the AIDS virus, so she was no longer wanted by her owners. Biju asked the crime lords how much money it would cost for him to buy her freedom.

The pimps took some time to calculate the amount. They had to assess how much money she used to make when she was forced to have sex with dozens of men each day. Then they lowered the price because of her illness. They came back to Biju and gave him their discounted price. It was $18.

It is hard for any of us to imagine someone placing so low of a price on a human life. But this is how the crime lords of Mumbai view street prostitutes. Had this woman been a younger, healthier virgin, her price would have been much higher. But in Kamathipura, women are cheap. They are just throwaways designed for the pleasure of men.

SEX IS NOT JUST ABOUT YOU

In the first century, when women had absolutely no human rights, the apostle Paul penned some revolutionary words about marriage that challenged old ideas about men and sexuality. He wrote in 1 Corinthians 7:2–4:

> But because of immoralities, each man is to have his own wife, and each woman is to have her own husband. The husband must fulfill his duty to his wife, and likewise also the wife to her husband. The wife does not have authority over her own body, but the husband does; and likewise also

the husband does not have authority over his own body, but the wife does.

We must remember that these words were written to the Corinthians, who lived in an ancient Greek city that was dominated by the temple of Aphrodite, the goddess of love and sexuality. The Bible scholar William Barclay points out that a thousand cult prostitutes descended from the Acropolis each evening to offer themselves to the many sailors and tradesmen who were passing through the seaside city. The place was like one giant Mediterranean brothel. "The very name Corinth was synonymous with debauchery," Barclay writes.[6]

Corinth was not that different from the Kamathipura district of Mumbai. Vile immorality was the rule here. The priestesses of Aphrodite engaged in continual sex with men in the vicinity of her altar, which featured a marble image of the naked goddess.[7] Corinth was a stronghold of wickedness, yet Paul was brave enough to go there to establish a beachhead to advance the gospel. And after he won his first converts, he worked hard to disciple them in the ways of righteousness. He had to reshape their old patterns of thinking.

Can you imagine how difficult it would have been to challenge the sinful traditions of Corinth? Men had been trained to be immoral. They had no concept of a holy marriage covenant. They satisfied their sexual needs with prostitutes anytime they pleased, even if they had a wife (or multiple wives) at home. They had been taught that the gods approved of them having multiple sex partners. Immorality was actually a part of the ritual in their idolatrous worship. Now, they are told that the true God actually wants them to abstain from adultery, fornication, homosexuality, and all other sex practices that are outside the boundaries of marriage.

When Paul addressed the Corinthians, he did more than reinforce the biblical standard of monogamy. After establishing that God wants one man and one woman to marry, he then explained that there is *equality* in the sexual relationship. He said the man has authority over his wife's body, and the wife has authority over the man's body. He acknowledged that both men and women have sexual needs, and husbands and wives have equal duties to each other. This was revolutionary in the first century—and it is still revolutionary in the minds of many men today who think sex is all about them and their needs.

Men in ancient Corinth believed their wives should provide sex for them whenever they demanded it. If their wives resisted, the husbands would force them to bed. And if the men wanted more sex, they could just go to the temple and find another pair of breasts and a vagina to please them. They had no consideration of women's feelings. Women had no intrinsic value; they were just body parts designed to help men find pleasure.

But Paul cut through this macho attitude and taught that wives are people too. They have worth and value as children of God. They also have sexual needs, and husbands are expected to meet them. Thus Paul laid the groundwork for a new view of marriage: a loving, equal partnership; tenderness; mutual communication; intimacy; and give-and-take.

Paul's teachings to the Corinthians and other similar biblical passages have helped me develop a healthy view of sexuality that guides my own marriage. Here are some key insights you must embrace if you want more than a one-sided sex life.

1. Sex is not just about intercourse.

Everybody knows that a man's sexual response is totally different from a woman's. Guys become aroused quickly, and then they are ready to go for it. Women, on the other hand, typically experience a more gradual arousal. Guys are built like sports cars—we can zoom from zero to eighty miles per hour in a few seconds. If it were totally up to us, we'd jump in bed and be finished in a minute flat. That's where we get the phrase, "Slam, bam, thank you, ma'am." For many men, sex is a race that involves these steps: (1) jump in bed, (2) get a quick erection, (3) make love for a few seconds until the fireworks go off, and (4) say good night and go to sleep. (And the most insensitive guys don't even say good night.)

So for many guys, sex is simply about "the big moment" of their orgasm. There's little or no foreplay, no real tenderness, and no communication. Women who are married to these sports car enthusiasts are usually extremely dissatisfied. Sex becomes something they simply endure—because their husbands are clueless about what they need.

You must learn to take it slow. Just because you have a powerful engine does not mean you must push the accelerator to the floor. To satisfy your wife you must focus on making sure she is fully aroused. She wants to be kissed, embraced, tenderly caressed, and touched in all the right places before intercourse begins. This will require you to put your own needs on the back burner so you can serve her. And learning to serve your wife sexually is an excellent way to tame your male ego. Paul told husbands in Ephesians 5:25–26:

> Husbands, love your wives, just as Christ also loved the church and gave Himself up for her, so that He might sanctify her, having cleansed her by the washing of water with the word.

This attitude of selfless servanthood should characterize every area of our marriages, but it should certainly be our rule in the bedroom. Your wife will not find sexual fulfillment if you are only interested in getting a quick jolt of excitement while she just lies there and tolerates you. That is selfish. You must put your wife's needs before yours. Be sure you smell good (ask her what cologne she prefers), and brush your teeth and use mouthwash before you climb in bed. Ask her how she wants to be touched. If you aren't a natural romantic, let her guide you.

Also, remember that foreplay does not start in the bedroom. Often it starts hours before, when you offer to help your wife clean the kitchen, take out the garbage, install a light bulb, or give her a neck rub on the couch after she's had a difficult day. If you begin your evening meal by barking orders at her or criticizing her, you have just soured the chances that you will have meaningful lovemaking that night. A woman wants to be loved throughout the day, not just when you decide it's time for a momentary thrill.

2. Sex is not just about your penis.

Let's face it: most of us guys are fixated on our sex organs. It's been that way since we hit puberty and discovered masturbation. During the teenage years, when we were shifting from the immaturity of childhood to the responsibility of adulthood, we viewed sex from a totally selfish perspective, and masturbation was the epitome of that selfishness. It's normal for young guys to discover sexual pleasure and to figure out how their bodies work, and we shouldn't condemn teenage boys for that. But once boys become men, they need to grow up and recognize that sex is not a one-man show anymore.

The apostle Paul, when teaching about godly love, said he "did away with childish things" after he became a man (1 Cor. 13:11). This certainly applies in the sexual area. Many guys need to put away their sophomoric attitudes about sex and stop acting like the frat boys from *Animal House*. Many men treat sex with their wives as a form of masturbation. When they were teens, they masturbated while looking at pictures of nude models in *Hustler*. When they got married, they just traded the racy photographs for a real woman. This makes a wife feel used. It is a denial of her personhood and makes her feel as if she is just an object with no feelings or desires of her own.

When I was a teenager I delved into some soft-core pornography that was available at the local drug store. One of the magazines advertised an inflatable plastic doll that was built like a voluptuous woman. It had a price tag, so I assume grown men actually purchased these lifeless sex toys. I can't think of anything sadder and more disgusting than a lonely man who has sex with a plastic woman—but I am sure some men do this today. What is even sadder is that some men view their wives as anatomically correct mannequins. This might explain why many men today insist that their wives get surgical breast implants; these men want their wives to look like the Barbie doll–style models they saw in a porn movie.

If you truly want to serve your wife sexually and put her needs above yours, then your priority should be that she will achieve an orgasm when you make love to her. Many men don't understand this. They think their wives should climax just because of the pleasure of intercourse.

You must realize that a woman's sexual response is especially enhanced by manual stimulation of her genitals, particularly her clitoris, the button-like projection of skin that is located at the top of the vagina. This small area of a woman's body is her most sensitive erogenous zone. If a husband tenderly rubs this part of his wife's body during foreplay, using some form of lubricant, the woman's clitoris will enlarge, her natural lubricants will moisten her vagina, and her sexual engine will be ready to accelerate.

You should not be disappointed to learn that most women cannot obtain a sexual climax simply from a man's thrusting actions. This is because the penis does not directly stimulate the clitoris during intercourse. However, when a man stimulates the clitoris with his hand while thrusting, the woman will easily achieve orgasm.

When sex therapists once asked women, "What do you think is the most important sex organ?" many of them said, "My husband's hand." Your wife loves your penis, I am sure, but she wants all of you. And she needs you to understand the intricate way God made her body so that you can bring her maximum sexual fulfillment.

Let's Talk About It

1. Why is the passage in 1 Corinthians 7:2–4 so revolutionary for the time it was written?
2. How would you describe the difference between a man's and a woman's sexual response?

3. If you are married, what are some ways that you could improve the way you are serving your wife sexually?

4. In what ways does our culture tell men to view women as sex objects?

---

3. Sex does not just revolve around your schedule.

I once prayed for a woman who came to a church altar in tears. She said her husband demanded sex from her at various times of the day, and if she protested he would rape her. This man, a professing Christian, also cited a Bible verse about how women should submit to their husbands.

That verse from Ephesians 5:22 says, "Wives, submit to your husbands as to the Lord" (NIV). It was written by Paul, who also wrote the passage in 1 Corinthians 7:2–4 about wives having authority over their husband's body. We must read both of these passages before we build a doctrine. Countless Christian women have been wounded because their husbands recited the passage in Ephesians and not the one in 1 Corinthians. We are supposed to seek the whole counsel of God, not just part of it.

As has already been stated in chapter 4, the biblical concept of submission does not give any husband the right to run roughshod over his wife, silence her, or deny her value as an equal partner in her marriage. And it certainly does not give a man the right to rape his wife. True biblical submission is never imposed, and it is not slavery; it is a woman's free choice.

Just before the Ephesians 5:22 passage, Paul says in verse 21: "Submit *to one another* out of reverence for Christ" (NIV, emphasis added). Implied in the construction of this passage is the concept that a woman's submission to her husband is done in the spirit of mutual submission. In other words, marriage is never a one-way street. And neither is a married couple's sex life.

So how do married couples determine the frequency of sex in their marriage? We all know many factors come into play here: The wife may be having her menstrual period. The husband may be too tired. One partner may have a headache. There may be young children sleeping in the bedroom. The couple may be getting older, when sexual urges change. It's up to a husband and wife to talk openly about their sex life. But you should never force sex on your wife if she is not physically or emotionally agreeable.

A wife, of course, must also have a servant attitude in the sexual area. She should never withhold sex just because her husband upsets her or use sex as a weapon to manipulate a decision. If her husband travels regularly, she should go out of her way to accommodate his sexual needs when he is home. If both partners adopt a policy of unselfish love, their sex lives will only grow richer and more meaningful as they grow old together.

4. Sex is a holy gift from God that you must protect.

Many guys I know first learned the facts about sexuality from a school classmate or from a lifeguard at the local beach. I knew a boy growing up who learned the facts of life when he discovered a stash of hard-core pornography in his brother's bedroom closet. That is sad, because fathers ought to be teaching their sons the facts of life. When we learn about sex from other sources, we think of it as dirty; when we learn about it from godly fathers, we respect it as a blessing from God that we should cherish.

Some of the best sex advice ever written was passed down from King Solomon to his son. He wrote in the Book of Proverbs:

> Drink water from your own cistern, running water from your own well. Should your springs overflow in the streets, your streams of water in the public squares? Let them be yours alone, never to be shared with strangers. May your fountain be blessed, and may you rejoice in the wife of your youth.

A loving doe, a graceful deer—may her breasts satisfy you always, may you ever be captivated by her love.

—PROVERBS 5:15–19, NIV

This passage compares godly marriage, and specifically sexuality, to a private garden spring. In ancient times, people had walled court-yards that sometimes included fountains. These were not for public consumption. They were walled to keep out intruders and to protect the water's freshness.

Godly sex in marriage is like that. It is walled garden, protected on all sides by the barriers of holiness and decency. It provides a husband and a wife with deep refreshment, and it is pure and joyful. Sex the way God intended is never dirty, painful, or shameful. It gives life. Doctors have even proven that regular sex provides a health benefit for couples, and an orgasm is an excellent way to relieve stress and keep the heart healthy.

But because of family dysfunction, lack of proper fathering, and cultural influences, many Christian men bring impurity into their marriages. They pollute the pure well of marital sex with toxic substances. They assume that just because they are Christians, they can do anything and everything they want to do in bed with their wife, yet the New Testament tells us in Hebrews 13:4:

Marriage is to be held in honor among all, and the marriage bed is to be undefiled; for fornicators and adulterers God will judge.

In other words, it is our responsibility to keep the marriage bed pure. We shouldn't allow anything into our sexual lives that would bring defilement. Yet over the years I have prayed for many women who suffered because their husbands did not heed this warning. Consider these examples:

- Some Christian men who struggle with pornography try to force their wives to watch adult videos so they can copy what is portrayed on film.
- Some men force their wives to perform sex acts (such as oral or anal sex) that their wives disapprove of.
- Some men want their wives to participate in bizarre sex games that involve bondage or torture or that require sex in public locations.
- Some men want to be extremely rough during sex and may force their wives to submit to profanity, spankings, or other forms of violence.
- Some husbands try to coerce their wives to agree to wife-swapping or three-way sex with another partner.

I knew of a man who demanded that his wife perform oral sex on him, and he told her that the Bible required her to do this because of the biblical injunction for wifely submission. Christians have differing opinions about oral sex, but one thing is clear: a husband never has the right to demand that his wife perform a sex act that she finds unpleasant or unreasonable. To force her into such submission is a defilement of the sanctity of marriage.

When a man and woman stand at a church altar and repeat their wedding vows, the minister declares that they have entered a covenant called "holy matrimony." The union has been sanctified. It is special in the eyes of God. Don't allow anything to degrade it. If you have unresolved sexual sin in your past, you will find it difficult to keep the wall of safety around your garden spring. You must determine that your marriage will stay pure, and you must trust in the grace of God to make you a good steward of this precious gift.

Let's Talk About It

1. Ephesians 5:22 says, "Wives, submit to your husbands as to the Lord" (NIV). How does this verse apply in the sexual area?
2. What does the author of Hebrews mean when he says to let the marriage bed be undefiled (Heb. 13:4)?
3. Think about your childhood and teenage years. Who first told you the facts about sexuality? Was it your father, mother, or some other person? How did this affect you later in life?
4. Are there any unresolved sexual issues in your life that you need prayer for? Are you comfortable talking to a pastor or mature Christian brother about this?

Let's Pray About It

For Married Men

Father, You said the pure in heart would see God. I want to walk in holiness. I confess to You any area of sexual impurity that I have brought into my marriage. I choose to renounce this sin. Cleanse me and forgive me. Help me to love my wife as an equal, to esteem her as precious and valuable, and to care more about her needs than I care about my own. Amen.

Let's Pray About It

For Single Men

Father, You said in Genesis 2:18 that it is not good for a man to be alone. I am trusting You to bring the woman of Your choice into my life. I confess to You any area of sexual impurity that has caused me to stumble. I don't want to bring that defilement into my future marriage. Cleanse me and forgive me. Help me to have a godly perspective of women and to view them as equals. And when I do find a wife, help me to love her, cherish her, and treasure her as a gift from God. Amen.

It's still hard for me to talk about the day I visited a shelter for children who were victims of a domestic-violence household. The kinds of abuse they had suffered, and what it had done to them physically and emotionally—I don't have words for what I saw. This has to stop.[1]
—MIKE CRAPO, IDAHO SENATOR

If the numbers we see in domestic violence were applied to terrorism or gang violence, the entire country would be up in arms, and it would be the lead story on the news every night.[2]
—MARK GREEN, WISCONSIN CONGRESSMAN

I've always thought a good lashing with a buggy whip would benefit you immensely.[3]
—CLARK GABLE AS RHETT BUTLER, TO SCARLETT O'HARA, IN *GONE WITH THE WIND*

Every man's a king, and I'm the king around here. And don't you forget it.[4]
—MARLON BRANDO AS STANLEY KOWALSKI IN *A STREETCAR NAMED DESIRE*

10 LIES

Lie #6

IT'S OK FOR A MAN TO HIT OR ABUSE A WOMAN.

E RARELY TALK about the issue of domestic violence. It's something that happens to other people in the secrecy of their own homes. It's rarely brought out into the open. That's mostly because men don't admit they abuse their wives or girlfriends (unless they are directly confronted), and women who are abused are just too ashamed to admit it. In many sad cases, abused women also tend to justify their partner's violence so they can stay in the relationship, no matter how much they or their children have suffered. Because of low self-esteem, they figure it's better to live with a man who beats them than to have no man at all.

The issue became a topic of national debate in the United States in 2009 after the pop singer and model known as Rihanna (her real name is Robyn Rihanna Fenty) canceled an appearance at the Grammy Awards ceremony.[5] It was later revealed that her then-boyfriend, hip-hop singer Chris Brown, had abused her and made criminal threats. A day later shocking photos were released that showed Rihanna battered and bruised. Her face and lips were grotesquely swollen, and she had cuts on her cheeks and forehead.[6]

Brown eventually pleaded guilty to felony assault and was sentenced to five years of probation. As the public outcry grew more intense, talk show host Oprah Winfrey dedicated her program to the topic of domestic violence and explored the reasons why women stay with abusive men, even when their lives are in danger. She looked into the cameras and pleaded with women to leave such situations. "If a man hits you once, he will hit you again," Oprah said.[7]

Yet in public discussions of the Rihanna case on the Internet, many fans of Brown, including many women, actually blamed Rihanna for the abuse. "She probably deserved it," or "She probably did something to make him mad," were typical responses.[8] One man posted this outrageous comment on a web forum: "Women enjoy being beaten up. I used to have a chick years ago who reminded me to beat her a week after I threatened to."[9]

How could anyone accept the idea that it's OK to punch, kick, bite, or slap a woman he is in a relationship with? And what happens to a woman's mind that conditions her to accept this treatment? Abuse is usually a learned behavior, and many abusive men grew up watching their fathers hit their mothers. Similarly, many women who tolerate abuse grew up in homes where they saw their mothers continually abused by husbands and boyfriends. Abuse starts a vicious cycle that continues through generations. Hurt breeds more hurt.

This kind of violence has actually become a quiet epidemic in our culture. Women are suffering incredible pain at the hands of their husbands, boyfriends, and sometimes even their fathers. It happens not only in secular culture but also in the church, even though the issue is rarely discussed from the pulpit. The facts don't lie. Consider these statistics:

- Around the world at least one in three women has been beaten, coerced into sex, or otherwise abused during her lifetime.[10]
- As many as 324,000 American women each year experience intimate partner violence during their pregnancy.[11]

- On average, more than three women are murdered by their husbands or boyfriends in the United States every day.[12]
- Domestic violence is the leading cause of injury to women between the ages of fifteen and forty-four in the United States.[13]
- Pregnant and recently pregnant women are more likely to be victims of homicide than to die of any other cause.[14]
- Approximately one in five female high school students reports being physically and/or sexually abused by a dating partner.[15]
- Three in four women (76 percent) who reported they had been raped and/or physically assaulted since age eighteen said that a current or former husband, cohabiting partner, or date committed the assault.[16]

In the United States, acceptance of abusive behavior is especially common in rap music. In 2007 two researchers, Chris Kubrin and Ronald Weitzer, studied the lyrics of hundreds of rap songs and presented their findings to the American Society of Criminology. They concluded that rap music most definitely promotes misogyny, or the hatred of women. The songs they studied contained these five common themes related to the abuse of women:

1. Derogatory naming and shaming of women
2. Sexual objectification of women
3. Distrust of women
4. Legitimization of violence against women
5. Celebration of prostitution and pimping[17]

Gangsta rap began in America's inner cities but is now popular among black, white, and Latino youth, even in middle-class and upper-class suburbs. Most rap singers are male, and their recordings offer a gritty portrayal of ghetto life that is punctuated by hard-core profanity, graphic depictions of illicit sex, and numerous references to illegal drugs. One of the most common themes of gangsta rap is the idea that a man proves he's tough when he abuses women or forces sex from them.

Artists such as Eminem, Snoop Dog, Notorious B.I.G., Three 6 Mafia, and many other rappers have recorded songs in this genre. Many of their profanity-laced songs include degrading references to women as sexually loose. Others offer graphic references to raping women, slapping them, and breaking their bones. One song even describes a man hitting a woman until her nose bleeds. Another popular song describes a man who sticks a gun down a woman's throat.

The common theme in many of these songs is the worthlessness of women, implying that they are only worth a quick moment of sexual pleasure and nothing else. In their report, Kubrin and Weitzer point out that while women are almost always denigrated in rap music, men who verbally or physically abuse women are praised by the rest of the men in the neighborhood. In some songs even gang rape is glorified.

Why should we be so surprised that domestic violence is a problem in our country when young people are listening to a steady diet of this garbage? At the very foundation of the rap music industry is the warped idea that a "real man" is tough and brutal and that he proves his manhood by raping or abusing as many women as possible.

THROW DOWN YOUR ROCKS

Jesus Christ lived in a culture that was extremely abusive toward women. In biblical times women had few human rights. All women were viewed as property, and they were denied access to education. Most were illiterate. They carried out the most menial and back-breaking of chores while men sat by and watched. They were expected to fulfill all domestic duties: fetch water, cook meals, have babies, tend to children, spin fabric, make clothes, sell their wares in the marketplace, and gather firewood. They were also expected to provide sex to their husbands whenever they demanded it, but men sometimes had multiple wives or other women on the side. Sex was always about meeting the man's needs.

A woman was never to question her husband's choices. Women were trained to stand quietly on the sidelines of society. They were veiled in yards of fabric. They were expected to stay indoors unless they traveled in groups. They sat in the back of the synagogues, sometimes behind a screen.

Men, including Jewish leaders, viewed women with disdain. Rabbis directed their teachings to men only. In fact, some rabbis recited this maxim as one of their traditions: "It is obscene to teach a woman from the Torah." They did not even believe that women had the right to learn from the Scriptures. Men in Israel thought all women were ignorant, deceitful, crafty, and immoral. If a rabbi saw a woman coming down the street toward him, he would cross to the other side. And in this patriarchal culture, men believed women were guilty until proven innocent.

Yet when we read the Gospels we see that Jesus Christ had a revolutionary view of women. He was like no other rabbi in Israel! Rabbis, for example, hated to talk about women, and they despised women's domestic life. What did Jesus do? He told parables that often mentioned women's work. He talked about a woman who lost a coin and about another woman who put yeast in three lumps of dough. Jesus included women in His ministry, and He addressed them directly; He even had women followers—even though no other rabbi in Israel believed in having women disciples.

Jesus also addressed the abuse of women in His culture—sometimes boldly and sometimes in subtle ways. Once He healed a woman who had been bleeding for twelve years. A woman with this kind of female problem would have been a social outcast, yet Jesus did not marginalize her. He praised her faith! Another woman, who was a prostitute, came to Jesus and began to wipe His feet with her tears. Any other rabbi would have rebuked this woman, but Jesus, again, praised her devotion in front of the Pharisees who judged her so harshly.

Widows were particularly vulnerable in biblical times. They were often desperately poor because without husbands they had no financial means to survive in a patriarchal society. Sometimes people even blamed a widow for her husband's death. Yet we often see Jesus coming to the aid of helpless women. Once, in the tiny village of Nain, He raised a widow's son to life because He felt compassion for the woman. In another instance He rebuked the Pharisees sharply because they "robbed widow's houses" by extorting them of their inheritance. (See Mark 12:40.) And once, while speaking to wealthy synagogue leaders, He praised a poor widow who only had one coin to give in the offering (and this woman had probably been treated unfairly by those male leaders).

Jesus modeled a totally different type of manhood when He walked the dusty roads of Israel. He was not weak or effeminate. But He modeled a strong yet gentle love that men (and women) had never seen. He was a bold preacher, yet He held children in His arms and blessed them. He fearlessly rebuked the Pharisees, yet He was secure enough in His masculinity to have women friends like Mary and Martha.

When Jesus went to Samaria, He sat down in broad daylight and carried on a lengthy theological discussion with a woman who had been divorced five times. Certainly no other rabbi would have done this, because men in those times did not speak with women in public—especially a woman with a questionable past. The Bible even says that Jesus's disciples were amazed that He was speaking with a woman. Yet Jesus broke the strict religious traditions of His society to fulfill a greater law—the law of love.

The Samaritan woman was an abused woman. Jesus looked into her heart and saw her pain, and by the power of the Holy Spirit He correctly described her situation. John 4:16–18 says:

> [Jesus] said to her, "Go, call your husband and come here." The woman answered and said, "I have no husband." Jesus said to her, "You have correctly said, 'I have no husband'; for you have had five husbands, and the one whom you now have is not your husband; this you have said truly."

We don't know the specifics of this woman's life story. But what we do know is that women did not have the right to a divorce in biblical times. The fact that she had five husbands means she had been divorced five times. This could have been because she was barren or because she could not produce a male heir. In that culture, men could legally divorce their wives for many reasons—even if they did not cook well.

Yet Jesus looked beyond all this pain and offered His kindness and affirmation to a love-starved woman. This is why she came to believe in Jesus as her Messiah—and why she found the courage to go to her village and tell all the men about Him.

In a male-dominated culture that marginalized and ignored women, Jesus celebrated women as individuals. He not only healed their bodies; He restored their dignity. He not only protected and affirmed them; He empowered them to speak. He showed them that God cared about them and had a plan for their lives.

Perhaps one of the best examples of Jesus's affirming view of women is found in the story of the woman accused of adultery in John 8. A group of angry scribes and Pharisees dragged a woman into the temple courtyard and claimed that the woman had been caught in moral compromise. John 8:4–7 says:

> They said to Him, "Teacher, this woman has been caught in adultery, in the very act. Now in the Law Moses commanded us to stone such women; what then do You say?" They were saying this, testing Him, so that they might have grounds for accusing Him. But Jesus stooped down and with His finger

wrote on the ground. But when they persisted in asking Him, He straightened up, and said to them, "He who is without sin among you, let him be the first to throw a stone at her.'"

These men obviously were not looking for true justice. Their accusation is quite suspicious, since they claimed to have caught this woman in the act, and yet they did not produce the man who was committing adultery with her. They also claimed that the Law demanded her execution—when actually the Old Testament Law required both the man and the woman to be stoned. This was an early biblical example of a kangaroo court!

No one knows what Jesus wrote in the dust. (Some have speculated that He was scribbling the names of the women these Pharisees had committed adultery with!) All we know is that when He finished writing and heavy conviction settled over the crowd, every one of these men dropped their rocks and walked away. Jesus stood there alone with the accused and said, "Woman, where are they? Did no one condemn you?" (v. 10).

This story shows us not only the love Jesus had for abused women and the justice He brought them, but it also shows that He has the power to change the hearts of abusive men. The love He demonstrated to this woman caused her accusers to drop their rocks, which symbolized the hardness of their own hearts.

Jesus still has the power to do this today. We all have hard hearts to some degree. Many men develop hard hearts because of the difficulties and disappointments they have faced in life. Some men are hard because of the way they were abused verbally by their fathers. This hardness becomes like a generational curse that is passed down through family lines. Some men are hard because they were taught that the only way to win in life is to fight people. And some men are abusive toward women because their fathers taught them that women are stupid, ignorant, or inferior and that men must dominate them.

No matter how hard our hearts are, Jesus will melt our pride when we stand before Him. Just as the Pharisees dropped their rocks when they saw the love of Christ defending a helpless woman, we too can experience a total turnaround in our attitude if we will allow His conviction to sink into our souls.

Let's Think About It

1. How do you feel when you read the lyrics of gangsta rap songs that degrade women?
2. Some men grow up believing that they are not truly masculine unless they are abusing women or forcing women into sex. What would you say to a man who has this mentality?
3. In what ways did Jesus model a different view of women than the men of His day?
4. When Jesus defended the woman who was caught in adultery, the men put down their rocks and walked away. Do you have any rocks to put down? Do you have any attitudes toward women that you need to repent of?

NOW LET'S GET PERSONAL!

Your attitudes toward women are determined partly by the way your family raised you and by what cultural and religious influences affected you the most. You may be completely free from all forms of gender prejudice. But it's also likely that somewhere inside you may harbor a sexist attitude, even if you were raised in a church! (Like racism, sexism often finds a haven in religious environments.) In third world countries sexism is blatantly obvious. In Western countries, where people may have more education, violence against women is still rampant, and gender-based discrimination is everywhere.

Are you willing to allow God's Word to change you if you have any wrong attitudes in your heart toward women? Below are some telltale signs that you may have an issue in this area. If you are brave enough to admit your weaknesses, check any boxes that might apply to you:

❑ You consider boys more "valuable" than girls.

❑ If you have a family, you favor your son(s) while keeping an emotional distance from your daughter(s).

❑ You tell jokes that are demeaning toward women.

❑ You think most women are stupid.

❑ If you are married, you don't include your wife in decision making.

❑ Your wife and/or children are usually afraid of you.

❑ You tend to negatively stereotype women (by saying such things as, "All women are bad drivers," or "All women are overly emotional").

❑ You tend to think of women only in terms of domestic duties, such as cooking, housecleaning, or laundry.

❑ You are uncomfortable around women who are successful in their careers.

❑ You secretly look at pornography, which causes you to view women as sex objects rather than individuals who are loved by God.

❑ You enjoy looking at pornography that depicts women in bondage or pain, or you have engaged in sexual practices that involved bondage.

❑ You have a problem with anger, especially when you are around your wife or girlfriend.

❑ You have broken objects or damaged property in the presence of your wife or girlfriend in order to make a statement.

❑ You have punched, kicked, slapped, scalded, or thrown an object at your wife or girlfriend.

❑ You have threatened to cause bodily harm to your wife or girlfriend.

❑ You have forced your wife or another woman to have sex with you.

If you have embraced any of these attitudes or have been involved in any of these behaviors, chances are you are not comfortable talking about them with anyone. You may feel anger as you read this list. You may even feel like throwing this book across the room! That's because sin hardens the human heart with pride, and proud people don't like to bring their mistakes into the light of God's truth. Jeremiah the prophet accurately described the human heart when he wrote:

> The heart is hopelessly dark and deceitful, a puzzle that no one can figure out. But I, God, search the heart and examine the mind. I get to the heart of the human. I get to the root of things. I treat them as they really are, not as they pretend to be.
>
> —Jeremiah 17:9, The Message

My challenge to you is simple: be willing to face the complexity of your own heart. Don't keep pretending. Ask God to search your attitudes. Be willing to repent from any wrong thoughts or actions.

A macho attitude, at its root, is really a spirit of pride. It says, "I am better than her. I will prove that I am better than her." Out of pride springs anger, hatred, and violence—which are total opposites of the tender love of God. This kind of pride has brought untold suffering to women throughout the world for centuries. Yet God is willing to forgive us when we simply acknowledge our sin and ask for His cleansing. King David, a man who had his own set of problems with sexual integrity, wrote these words in Psalm 32:1–2:

> How blessed is he whose transgression is forgiven, whose sin
> is covered! How blessed is the man to whom the LORD does
> not impute iniquity, and in whose spirit there is no deceit!

This is what is so amazing about our God. When we turn to Him in humble repentance, admitting our wrong without any excuses or cover-ups, He forgives us totally. And He also extends to us the inward grace to change. You may have been a prideful man in the past, but God is not finished with you yet. He wants to change you into the very likeness of His Son. True masculinity is not about maintaining a "tough guy" image; it requires you to reflect the love, gentleness, compassion, and humility of Christ.

If you have been involved in any form of abusive behavior, especially physical or sexual abuse, you must talk openly about this with a pastor, mature friend, or Christian counselor. Don't procrastinate, because men who abuse women often go back into hiding after their sin has been exposed. You will be tempted to hide your sin from everyone you know, but the only way to find true deliverance is to bring your sin out into the open. If you are married and you have been abusing your wife, she will also need to seek pastoral advice and counsel.

Let's Think About It

1. After examining the list of "telltale signs" listed in this chapter, are you willing to admit that you have struggled in one or more of these areas? Which ones?

2. Why do you think these types of attitudes or actions grieve God?

3. Besides yourself, whom else have you hurt by these attitudes or actions? Be specific.

4. Are you willing to ask a friend or your men's group to pray for you now about these issues?

Let's Pray About It

If you have abused a woman in any way—physically, emotionally, or sexually—ask another brother to pray with you as you say these words:

Father, forgive me for all the pain I have caused. I repent for my cruel behavior. I am sorry for the way I treated _____ (say the name—or names—of the women you have hurt). Please deliver me from all my pride, unforgiveness, and anger, and pull out the root of abuse in my heart. I receive Your cleansing from all my sin, and I ask You to give me the grace to be a protector of women instead of an abuser, in Jesus's name. Amen.

Ships that pass in the night, and speak to each other in passing,
Only a signal shown, and a distant voice in the darkness;
So on the ocean of life, we pass and speak one another,
Only a look and a voice, then darkness again and a silence.[1]
—HENRY WADSWORTH LONGFELLOW

The whole conviction of my life now rests upon the belief
that loneliness, far from being a rare and curious phenom-
enon, peculiar to myself and to a few other solitary men,
is the central and inevitable fact of human existence.[2]
—THOMAS WOLFE

One may have a blazing hearth in one's soul,
and yet no one ever comes to sit by it.[3]
—VINCENT VAN GOGH

Many men grew up in a masculine vacuum—they grew up
with fathers who were non-nurturing, uncommunicative, or
absent a lot of the time. This left them in a literal no-man's
land of confusion about how to express authentic maleness.[4]
—PASTOR BILL HYBELS IN HIS BOOK *HONEST TO GOD*

---

10 LIES

REAL MEN DON'T NEED CLOSE MALE FRIENDSHIPS.

I'M OLD ENOUGH to remember the Marlboro Man. He was one of the most famous images ever used in advertising, and he successfully convinced millions of men around the world that they must smoke cigarettes, preferably on the open range, in order to prove their masculinity. The Marlboro Man was ruggedly handsome and was always dressed in jeans, leather chaps, and a cowboy hat. He was sometimes holding the reins of his horse and was often shown looking out over a vast western prairie as he lit up his smoke.

And he was always, always alone.

The message coming from this icon was subliminal but compelling: If you want to be a real man, you need to act like this guy. He's burly. He doesn't say much. He doesn't need anyone. He just mounts his steed and rides into the sunset by himself. In most of the ads, a single photo of the broad-shouldered, sun-baked cowboy was usually featured without any text. In a few exceptions a caption read, "Come to where the flavor is."

The Phillip Morris tobacco company invented the Marlboro image in 1954 to sell their line of cigarettes to men. They struck a gold mine.

Within a few decades this hard-edged cowboy became one of the most famous fictitious characters of all time. Ironically, three of the models who posed for the advertising campaigns died of lung cancer because they used the product they sold to the gullible public.[5] Tobacco advertising was banned from the airwaves in 1971 in the United States,[6] so after that the Marlboro Man was only seen in magazines. Within a few more years, as the negative effects of smoking became more obvious, Marlboro cigarettes came to be known as "cowboy killers."[7]

The Marlboro man ad campaign was certainly not the first time popular media peddled the notion of the "real man" as a tough, independent loner. He's depicted in everything from comic books and films to classic literature and rock music. For some odd reason, guys are attracted to the idea that we are our best when we are alone—and even better if we are disguised.

I grew up watching a steady stream of these macho men, from the masked Lone Ranger and Zorro characters on television to the tough-talking US Marshall Rooster Cogburn in *True Grit*, played by the ultimate tough guy, John Wayne. Then there was novelist F. Scott Fitzgerald's Jay Gatsby of *The Great Gatsby*, a mysterious millionaire who cashed in on all the prosperity that the Roaring Twenties had to offer but never found true love. Meanwhile the dashing spy character James Bond proved (or so we were led to believe) that you don't have to settle down; you can jet-set around the world, unravel terrorist plots, kill all the bad guys, and have your pick of beautiful women without marrying any of them.

Comic book superheroes especially emphasized the notion that real men are tough on the outside and yet mysteriously lonely. If you study the plotlines of Superman, Spider-man, Iron Man, or Batman, you find average guys who hide behind masks and tight-fitting uniforms. Most of them live alone with torturous secrets, and they rarely if ever reveal their true identities. Most of them have only one weakness. They are known for their façades. Yet they always seem to save the day and impress the women while their superhuman accomplishments are praised in the newspapers.

Through all of these media creations we are taught that manhood is about the exterior. A real man creates a wall around himself, like protective body armor. He uses his muscular strength to create an illusion of power, then he hides behind that force and never lets anyone see who he really is. And these guys don't face their emotions. Batman, for example, either retreated to his bat cave or just climbed on the roof of a skyscraper at night and brooded in silence. Superman did his sulking in an ice cave near the North Pole. And even though the Lone Ranger had a companion, his Native American friend Tonto didn't say much.

I was captivated by this superhero image when I was a boy. Most young guys are. When you are nine years old, you feel skinny and vulnerable in an adult world, so the thought of having Captain America's giant biceps or Superman's height or Spider-man's agility is empowering. When a boy grows into a man and realizes he struggles with flaws and weaknesses, the thought of hiding his secrets behind a mask, long cape, and vinyl body suit is appealing. No one ever has to know the real you.

But there is a huge problem with this concept. Like Batman or the Marlboro Man, the strong, silent superhero is an illusion. In real life, the Marlboro Man had an addiction that created a hacking cough and other serious health problems. He was not as strong as he appeared, and in the end he died in a cancer ward. As far as the superheroes of comic book lore, they are a total fantasy, like Hercules of Greek mythology or the James Bond of modern movies. Guys like that don't exist. Real men don't wear masks or body suits. Real men have to face the world, take responsibility, pay bills, open their hearts, feel other people's pain, and admit their own weaknesses.

Real men are not like the Jedi knights of *Star Wars*, who took a pledge to keep their emotions hidden. Real men love. Real men have to show their feelings.

And real men aren't loners. They have a deep need for relationships. Real men build genuine friendships with each other. Yet if you look around at today's busy culture, even among Christian guys, you find that most men never allow their relationships to go beyond a superficial discussion about sports, weather, or the latest software upgrade.

David Smith, author of the book *The Friendless American Male*, says this male friendship deficit has reached a crisis point. Speaking to men Smith writes, "Few of us value close, interpersonal relationships, and fewer still seem willing to invest the time and emotional energy necessary for the development of closeness. The fragmentation of community life; corporate pressures; the breakdown of the extended and nuclear family; the drive for success; and the rate of mobility have all taken a tremendous toll on the numbers of intimate friendships we acquire and sustain."[8]

Shallow Men, Sad Men

While our culture tells us that real men are independent loners, the Bible shows us that the lonely man is actually part of the brokenness of sinful human nature. At the very beginning of Creation, God declared to Adam, "It is not good for the man to be alone" (Gen. 2:18). God has always wooed man away from his inclination to be proud and self-sufficient; He calls us into authentic fellowship and deep intimacy.

But sin always brings alienation. Immediately after the fall of Adam and Eve, when pride and selfishness became the rule, the perfection of the marriage relationship was ruined. The husband and wife were estranged; then, in the next cruel scene in Genesis, brothers turned on each other. Cain killed Abel and then ran away to the land of Nod to become a lonely fugitive. Friendlessness and isolation became a normal part of his existence, and he passed this on to his descendants.

When God confronted Cain for killing his brother, He pronounced this curse over him in Genesis 4:12: "When you cultivate the ground, it will no longer yield its strength to you; you will become a *vagrant* and a *wanderer* on the earth" (emphasis added). The Hebrew words for "vagrant" (*nuwa*) and "wanderer" (*nuwd*) can imply shameful mourning as well as aimless wandering. The words can also mean "shaking," as in fearful trembling. These terms provide a more accurate picture of the true "Marlboro Man." Under this tough, manly exterior is a very scared guy.

Cain ran to the wilderness because he was ashamed of his past and couldn't face his true identity as a cold-blooded, jealous murderer. Sin is a powerful reality; the separation from God that sin causes always cripples a man's ability to build genuine relationships. It makes him a lonely wanderer. And unless a man allows Jesus Christ to repair his sin-sick condition, he will become emotionally homeless. He will lack the stability of relationships and instead float here and there, pretending to be strong when inside he is seething with pain.

Let's face it: there's a little bit of Cain in all of us. It's why men hide behind their careers and accomplishments; it's why men go to bars at "happy hour" to drown their sorrows in alcohol; it's why men pretend to have happy marriages while carrying on illicit affairs. It's why even some Christian men put on their spiritual bodysuits and act the part of a man of God when they actually are trembling with fear on the inside, afraid someone will discover they aren't the perfect husbands, fathers, and employees they pretend to be.

Let's Talk About It

1. What cultural influences (movies, TV shows, comic books, or music) shaped your idea of a "real man"?
2. Why do you think men tend to have a difficult time building authentic friendships?
3. Be honest: Do you ever feel lonely? If so, is this because you don't have enough close friends?

Besides this ugly spiritual root of sinful nature, there are many other obvious reasons why men don't develop close relationships with other guys. Here are the most common:

1. We have a flawed concept of our heavenly Father.

God made us in His image, and He is an emotional God. He feels intense love, compassion, mercy, and forgiveness, as well as anger and protective jealousy—and He does not bury these emotions. Yet many men grow up imagining that God is an austere old judge with a long white beard; they think God is always frowning and ever ready to zap them with a lightning bolt if they step out of line. But this is not the God of the Bible!

Actually, it was a pagan god—the Greek deity Zeus—who was so judgmental and hot-tempered that he carried an arsenal of thunderbolts to unleash on his subjects. The same could be said of Baal, the fickle god of prosperity and fertility who was sometimes worshiped by the children of Israel when they were in a backslidden state. They were constantly tempted to trade the true God for this angry idol.

One of my favorite verses about the true nature of God is Zephaniah 3:17, which describes the extravagant way He shows His love to us:

> The LORD your God is in your midst, a victorious warrior.
> He will exult over you with joy, He will be quiet in His love,
> He will rejoice over you with shouts of joy.

Is this how you view God? Do you imagine Him as a strong yet compassionate Father who tenderly caresses His children, sings to them, and bounces them on His knee? Or is your God cold, distant, impossible to please, and always upset? How you see God will directly determine the level of true joy in your life and whether you feel free to express your emotions.

Notice that in this Old Testament description of God, He is both strong (as a warrior) and extravagantly emotional (exulting in joy). There is nothing inconsistent about these two qualities. Strong men can be secure enough to show their true feelings, but if we haven't come to know God in a deeply personal way we will never find this kind of emotional liberation.

2. We did not see emotional freedom modeled by our fathers or other men.

I grew up in a genteel white culture in Alabama and Georgia, where men were expected to be "Southern gentlemen." When men got together to talk, their discussions usually centered around football, politics, or the weather. When they went to church, they dressed in suits. Life was about rules and traditions.

In this type of religious culture people tend to focus on externals; they live life on the surface. They rarely open up their lives or talk about personal issues. Everything is superficial. They may be hurting inside, but they will never open up. They certainly don't talk about their dark secrets. People's problems never become a part of conversation until they end up in the hospital or die.

When I was young I would sometimes sit with a group of older male relatives and listen to their conversations over big family dinners. They talked about the Great Depression, old-fashioned cars, fishing trips, and one-room schoolhouses they attended in the rural South. Years later I would learn that some of these men struggled with alcoholism, but such things were never talked about openly. Men were expected to wrestle alone with their private demons; family problems were only whispered about.

3. We are too proud to admit we have needs.

A Jewish leader named Nicodemus came to Jesus to find out if He was really the Messiah, yet the Bible says Nicodemus came to Jesus at night because he was afraid of the other Pharisees (John 3:2). He could not bear to let his peers know he was talking to their rival. The Pharisees were smug in their religious pride and would not admit they needed a Savior. Nicodemus didn't want his colleagues to know that he needed more than his superficial religiosity could provide.

Jesus, of course, explained to Nicodemus that in order for him to find the truth he must be "born again" (John 3:3). He must start life over completely, leaving his old ways behind. Jesus was making it clear that the only way to begin a faith journey with Christ is to take the path of true repentance and conversion. And there is no way we can be born again if we don't humble ourselves, admit our need for salvation, and seek forgiveness from God for the way we have lived apart from Him.

The journey of faith, then, begins with an admission of weakness! No wonder so many men have a difficult time beginning the process.

Many guys suffer from the Nicodemus complex. We care too much about what other guys think to admit we are in need of salvation. Like the Pharisees, who loved to wear their long robes and use fancy religious titles, we pretend we have it all together. Yet Jesus was very blunt when He addressed the prideful Jewish leaders of His day. He rebuked them sternly because they were covered with the thick armor of pride. He even called them "whitewashed tombs" (Matt. 23:27) because they covered their sins and insecurities with prideful self-sufficiency.

What is more masculine: to act tough and independent or to show weakness by repenting openly for your failures? Jesus always honored the honest man who admitted his weakness, no matter how poor he was or how emotional he became in his display of repentance. If you are not quick to repent when the Holy Spirit convicts you or when your sin is challenged by someone else, then your heart has already become dangerously hard.

God loves His sons to be tough when it comes to boldness and fearlessness. But He never called us to be hard, angry, or mean-spirited. That is not the character of Christ. Hardness of heart is a sign that we are out of fellowship with God and that we don't have His presence in our lives. Isaiah 66:1–2 says:

Thus says the LORD, "Heaven is My throne, and the earth is My footstool. Where then is a house you could build for Me? And where is a place that I may rest? For My hand made all these things, thus all these things came into being," declares the LORD. "But to this one I will look, to him who is humble and contrite of spirit, and who trembles at my Word."

The word *contrite* actually means "ground into a powder." This is the kind of heart God looks for in a man. He wants us to be sensitive to the promptings of His Holy Spirit and to the needs of others. We must be quick to repent the moment He convicts us that we have said an unkind word, mistreated a colleague, hurt our spouse, or grieved God with an unclean thought.

Is your heart sensitive and pliable? Or does God have to bang you over the head with a two-by-four to get your attention? Are you humble enough to receive correction from a sermon, a brother's gentle reproof, or your wife's counsel? Or does God have to put you in difficult circumstances in order to speak to you? A real man of God is not hard-hearted or stubborn. If you have been walking in pride, ask God to crush your pride and make you contrite.

4. We prefer to medicate our emotional pain.

God created us with the capacity for emotional release. He gave us mouths so we could talk openly about our struggles. He gave us tear ducts so we could cry when necessary. He gave us ears so that we could listen to others when they are hurting. He gave us arms and hands to be able to soothe and embrace our brothers when they are dealing with grief or tragedy.

But what happens when we don't use these outlets? What happens when we turn off all our emotional valves so that all our feelings are blocked and buried? The human soul was not created to absorb life's pain year after year like this. Pain must be processed; it cannot be stuffed inside the recesses of our hearts. If a man experiences trauma, grief, relationship breakdown, guilt, unforgiveness, or other forms of emotional hurt, he must be able to talk about his struggles and apply the healing of Christ. If he doesn't do this, his wounds will be internalized, and his pain will spread like a sickness. When a man buries his problems, he must find something to numb the pain.

That's why so many men become addicted to things like alcohol, nicotine, marijuana, illegal drugs, or prescription medicines. These substances offer temporary relief because they alter reality. Nobody smokes a cigarette because they like the smell of toxic smoke. It's filthy! No man drinks vodka because he likes the flavor. It tastes like airplane fuel! He drinks hard liquor because it makes him drunk—and when he is intoxicated he can't feel the weight of his problems. It is a useless attempt to escape life for a few hours.

This is also the reason some men become addicted to pornography. The temporary sexual excitement that porn triggers in the human brain is like a powerful drug. The more hard-core the porn, the more serious the addiction it can cause. Porn can temporarily numb a man's pain, just like alcohol. But the next day always arrives, always with a letdown and a hangover. Porn proves to be a pitiful substitute for real sexual intimacy.

Men medicate their pain for many reasons: financial stress, the loss of a child, divorce, a moral failure, or unresolved family problems. And what happens when they are drunk or high? Often their personalities change. They can become belligerent and even dangerously violent. The emotions they buried suddenly resurface with a vengeance.

The Bible actually acknowledges that alcohol is a deceptive form of medication. Proverbs 31:4–7 says:

> It is not for kings, O Lemuel, it is not for kings to drink wine, or for rulers to desire strong drink, for they will drink and forget what is decreed, and pervert the rights of all the afflicted. Give strong drink to him who is perishing, and wine

to him who whose life is bitter. Let him drink and forget his poverty and remember his trouble no more.

This passage is not endorsing the use of liquor as an emotional sedative. But it implies that a person who does not have access to the love and mercy of God will probably seek solace in a bottle. Life is hard, and if we don't give our brokenness to the Lord, it is difficult to find healing anywhere else.

We really only have one viable option, and that is to take our pain to Christ, who bore our pain in His own body when He was crucified. When Jesus was dying on the cross, the Bible tells us that the Roman guards offered Him some wine that was "mixed with gall" (Matt. 27:34). Yet Jesus refused to drink this mixture. Tradition tells us that condemned prisoners often were given this bitter narcotic substance to help deaden the pain of crucifixion.

Yet Jesus refused to numb His pain. Why? Because He knew He could not run from the cross—He had to endure it for us. He had already surrendered His will completely to His Father when He prayed at the Garden of Gethsemane, "Father, if it is possible, let this cup pass from Me; yet not as I will, but as You will" (Matt. 26:39). Jesus had already chosen to drink the cup of suffering; therefore He refused the cup of bitter wine that had the power to numb His pain temporarily. He refused the quick fix. He rejected the easy way out. He made this difficult choice for you and me so that we could find true healing in our souls.

In light of Christ's suffering for us, how foolish it is for us to try to drown our sorrows and pain in substances that have no real power to help us. No amount of beer, rum, vodka, whiskey, gin, nicotine, cocaine, marijuana, LSD, methamphetamines, glue, Quaaludes, Valium, or any other substance can relieve sin's pain like the blood of Jesus does.

5. We think it is feminine to show our emotions.

Some men were taught as boys never to cry or to show affection. Often boys are also ridiculed by classmates if they cry or appear emotionally weak. This teaches a boy that in order to be a man he must put an iron lid on his feelings.

In the 1984 film *Red Dawn*, the United States is invaded by Soviet armies, and World War III begins.[9] A group of teenagers from a small town in Colorado escape the communist takeover and hide in the mountains, but after a few months they venture back into town to check on their families. Two of the boys find their father in a Soviet prison camp, and they talk to him through a barbed-wire fence. Both of the boys begin to cry after they see evidence of torture on their dad's face.

"Don't you dare cry," the father says sternly. "Let it turn to hate."

While *Red Dawn* offered a totally implausible plot, the father's advice accurately reflects the attitude of many American men. If they are tempted to feel grief, sadness, or affection, they slam the lid on their emotions and try to remain stoic. Their idea of a real man is a guy who has successfully disengaged with his feelings by stuffing them so far inside that they will never, ever be discovered.

They also believe that the only acceptable emotion a man can display is anger and hatred. This is a cruel, demonic lie. Satan is the ultimate crime boss, and his kingdom is built on bitterness, resentment, revenge, strife, jealousy, and murder. Meanwhile, God's kingdom is built on mercy, forgiveness, compassion, kindness, gentleness, tenderness, loyalty, and unconditional love. Those are not sissy character qualities—they are the qualities of our heavenly Father.

If you think there is anything manly about anger, violence, or brutality, then your mind has been warped by the devil himself. You must ask the Lord to renew your mind with His Word.

6. We have a fear of being labeled "homosexual."

In some cultures, men are profusely affectionate with each other, and there are no sexual overtones to their hugging, kissing, or touching. In Italian families, for example, men kiss each other on the cheek, and there is no social stigma attached to this. In Nigeria, where homosexuality is rarely discussed and few people even know a gay person, men are comfortable holding hands as they walk down the street. There is nothing sexual about this; it is simply viewed as a normal display of friendship.

During my first visit to Nigeria several years ago a pastor grabbed my hand as we were walking through the streets of Lagos. He wanted everyone to know I was his friend, and he also wanted me to feel safe in the crowded downtown district. I must admit it felt awkward to me at first. I was sure people were going to laugh at us or label us gay. That didn't happen. Now when I visit Nigeria I am comfortable grabbing my male friends' hands. It makes me feel a deeper sense of brotherly comradeship with them.

Of course, I would not feel comfortable doing this in my own country because our culture has sexualized hand holding. But as I have allowed the Lord to heal my emotions and give me a greater capacity to love, I find it easier to express pure, godly affection to my brothers in Christ. All of us need to discover this freedom.

Jesus was actually very affectionate with His male disciples. This is especially obvious in the writings of John, who referred to himself in his Gospel account as the disciple "whom Jesus loved" (John 13:23). After Jesus washed His disciples' feet—which was an unusual display of humility and affection—He reclined at the Passover table with them, and they shared their last meal together. During the Seder, John was comfortable enough in his friendship with Jesus to lay his head on His teacher's chest. *The Message* Bible says John had "his head on [Jesus'] shoulder."

The deeply affectionate friendship John had with Jesus actually shaped his theology. He says this about the incarnate Son of God:

> What was from the beginning, what we have heard, what we
> have seen with our eyes, what we have looked at and touched
> with our hands, concerning the Word of Life.... What we
> have seen and heard we proclaim to you also, so that you too
> may have *fellowship* with us; and indeed our *fellowship* is with
> the Father, and with His Son Jesus Christ.
>
> —1 JOHN 1:1, 3, EMPHASIS ADDED

John affirms here that he not only knew Jesus's words but that he actually touched Him. Jesus was not just a concept or an ideology to John. He was a man, in flesh and blood, who embodied the fullness of Deity. John's experience with Christ was not just intellectual or spiritual; he hugged Jesus, laid his head on His chest, and listened to His heartbeat. He and Jesus were intimate friends in the purest sense.

In John's first epistle he introduces the Greek word *koinonia*, or "fellowship," to describe not only close communion we have with Jesus but also the spiritual bond we can have with each other. *Koinonia* literally means "communion through intimate participation." It implies deep sharing and close personal contact. This is part of our spiritual inheritance as Christians; because we have Christ in our hearts, we feel an unusual sense of closeness to other believers.

As a man of God, you should not be afraid of *koinonia*. You should feel the freedom to express brotherly affection to other men. If you don't, it may be because of fear or pride that you have created emotional walls in your soul. God wants you to be free emotionally so you can show genuine love to others.

You may actually need to be hugged in order to discover this freedom. There have been times when I felt the Lord direct me to hug a brother when I was praying for people at the altar of a church. In some cases these men had fathers who were either abusive or distant, and they struggled to relate to God as Father. When I would hold such men in my arms, often they would begin sobbing for several minutes. They received a powerful emotional healing through a simple embrace.

If we want to give this kind of freedom to other men, we must first receive it. God wants you to be a channel of His love.

Let's Talk About It

1. Would you say that your father was emotionally open or closed? How do you think this affected you?

2. God is described as a Father. When you think of your relationship with God, do you view Him as an affectionate, loving Father, or more of a rigid, angry disciplinarian? Why do you think you view God in this way?

3. The Bible says God draws near to the person who is humble and broken. When you examine your life, can you identify any areas of pride or hard-heartedness? Is it easy for you to apologize to others or admit when you have made a mistake?

4. Is it easy for you to show love to others, either through words or physical affection? Why or why not?

RETURNING TO RELATIONAL CHRISTIANITY

Jesus came into a very sterile religious culture shaped by legalistic Jewish leaders. The rabbis of Jesus's day believed that the only way they could be holy was to stay away from people they considered sinful or spiritually unclean. Their faith was totally focused on externals; they believed they could win God's approval by eating the right foods, following all the laws of the Old Testament (in their own power), and staying away from anything or anyone that might contaminate them.

Rabbis were quite obsessed with physical hygiene. In one scene in Mark 7, the Bible says that they criticized Jesus because His disciples did not wash their hands in the proper ceremonial fashion before eating. These leaders actually believed they could grow closer to God by washing their hands. They didn't understand that they should have been more conscious of the inward condition of their heart.

Rabbis in Jesus's culture had a long list of people they would not touch. They were not affectionate with children because they felt women should be attending to them. They viewed women as unclean, especially during the time of their menstrual cycle. They would never eat near people they considered sinners. They stayed far away from foreigners. And they would never go near a leper or a dead body because they feared disease. Their rule in life was "Don't touch!"

Yet what did Jesus do? He modeled the incarnational love of God by going out of His way to touch the untouchable. He held children in His arms and blessed them. He healed a bleeding woman. He sat down in a public place to speak with a divorced Samaritan woman. He touched lepers and healed them, and He ate with tax collectors and sinners. He allowed a sinful woman, probably a prostitute, to wash His feet with her hair. And He laid His hands on many, many sick people who would have been considered ceremonially unclean by other Jews.

Jesus also rebuked the Pharisees because of their legalistic elitism. When they got upset about His disciples' dirty hands, He said to them:

> Rightly did Isaiah prophesy of you hypocrites, as it is written: "This people honors Me with their lips, but their heart is far from Me. But in vain do they worship Me, teachings as doctrines the precepts of men." Neglecting the commandment of God, you hold to the tradition of men.
>
> —MARK 7:6–8

The Pharisees had their priorities and values all mixed up. They thought true holiness was found in staying away from "dirty" people. Yet Jesus told them that this religious attitude actually invalidated the real commandment of God—which is to share His love with others!

Jesus showed us that Christianity, in its very essence, requires touch. True faith is not just an intellectual doctrine about God's existence or His nature. Real Christianity is about a God who loved us so much that He became human flesh and came to Earth to dwell among us (John 1:14). God did not just give us nice words; He did not just write, "I love you," or "I forgive you," in the sky. He sent His Son to wrap His arms around us.

When you have been truly touched by the love of God, the message of the gospel will be much more to you than Bible verses or doctrines. Biblical teaching is important, but you will not know God in His fullness if you only know intellectual information about Him. Faith must go beyond your head to touch your heart.

Wherever the message of the gospel goes, it does more than give people an intellectual faith. It imparts true love because God is love. A heart that has been changed by Christ suddenly loves others. And a person who has been transformed by the gospel of Jesus will have the supernatural capacity to demonstrate God's love in an extravagant way.

The apostle Paul demonstrated this remarkable love in his ministry to the churches he guided in the first century. Although he himself had been a Pharisee before his conversion, and he practiced all the traditions of Jewish legalists (including ritual hand-washing and aloofness from tax collectors and "sinners"), he adopted a radically new method of ministry after he became a minister of the gospel. Saul the stoic Pharisee became Paul the affectionate lover of people.

For example, he compared his love for the Thessalonian church to a mother's affection. He wrote, "But we proved to be gentle among you, as a nursing mother tenderly cares for her children" (1 Thess. 2:7). He told the Philippians, "I have you in my heart....I long for you with all the affection of Christ Jesus" (Phil 1:7–8). Paul was almost slobbering in his profuse love for his New Testament flock. He urged them to greet each other with a "holy kiss," and he sometimes wept when he prayed for the churches.

When Paul left Ephesus for Jerusalem, the leaders of that church suspected that they might not see him again. So when Paul prayed for them as they knelt on the beach, the Bible says they wept aloud and embraced Paul "and repeatedly kissed him" (Acts 20:36–38). The most influential leader of New Testament Christianity was comfortable with this type of emotional display. Why? Because a man who has been truly freed by Christ is able to love without emotional reservation.

We also see this affection evident in Paul's close relationship with his ministry colleague, Timothy. Paul discipled and trained this young convert and eventually called him his "true child in the faith." Much of the New Testament was written against a backdrop of Paul's and Timothy's friendship. While Paul wrote two epistles directly to Timothy, Paul and Timothy together sent the epistles of 2 Corinthians, Philippians, Colossians, 1 and 2 Thessalonians, and Philemon.

More than one-third of the entire New Testament came from these two men, who shared a unique ministry bond. And Paul's last words to the church, written from a cold dungeon in the time of Emperor Nero, were addressed to Timothy. It was in that epistle that he told his beloved son, "Make every effort to come to me soon" (2 Tim. 4:9).

We cannot ignore this intense relational aspect of genuine Christianity. The authentic gospel is not just about taking a nice message of hope to people. It is not just about building churches or preaching sermons or hosting big meetings. Real Christianity involves deep, lasting relationships with the people God brings into our lives. He has called us to do ministry together, and the affection we feel for each other is a testimony of the power of Christ's love.

I heard a man of God say many years ago that every Christian guy needs three kinds of relationships in his life: (1) a Paul, (2) a Barnabas, and (3) a Timothy. What he meant by this was simple. Pauls are mentors and spiritual fathers. Barnabases are peers or close friends who are on our same spiritual maturity level with us. Timothys are younger men who ask us to disciple them.

In recent years I have had the joy of making friends on all three of these levels. These relationships are more valuable to me than riches, and I would not trade them for anything. When it comes to Pauls, I have several older, mature men of God who see me as a spiritual son. They are my role models, but not just from a distance. They spend time with me, pray for me, offer counsel and coaching, and genuinely care about my family and my ministry.

I also have several Barnabases who are what I would call true bosom friends. I am able to share with them my deepest struggles and concerns. We hold each other accountable regarding our temptations and weaknesses. One of my closest friends knows how to ask me the "hard questions" so that I can keep my life sexually pure. Every man needs a friend who will watch his back!

And in recent years I have been blessed to have several Timothys in my life. Some of them travel with me when I minister in churches or when I go on mission trips to foreign countries. I don't take these young men along so they can carry my luggage (in fact, I discourage this). Rather, I pull them alongside me and ask them to help me pray with people at the end of a church service. I make them feel they are a valuable part of our ministry team. I want them to see Christ in my life. I pray with them and offer counsel when needed, but I mostly share my life in an authentic way.

Having these kinds of genuine relationships with men has been a great area of fulfillment in my life—and I believe it is part of every Christian man's spiritual inheritance. God does not want you to be lonely or isolated. He wants to bless you with authentic relationships.

Let's Talk About It

1. Describe the religion of the Pharisees. Why did Jesus rebuke the Pharisees when they criticized His disciples for not washing their hands?

2. Jesus touched people in an authentic way when the Pharisees never touched people. In what ways can you touch more people for Christ?

3. Paul was a Pharisee at one time, but he changed radically after his conversion. In what ways did Paul the apostle model relational Christianity?

4. Every man should have a Paul, a Barnabas, and a Timothy in his life. Can you list men in your life who fit in these categories?

Let's Pray About It

Father, I don't want to live a closed life. I don't want to be alienated or lonely. Please open my heart so that I can have genuine, authentic relationships—not only with my wife but also with the men around me. Remove any pride, religiosity, or fear that keeps me in emotional bondage. Open my heart so I can show Your love to others. Amen.

I have let my family down, and I regret those transgressions with all of my heart. I have not been true to my values and the behavior my family deserves. I am not without faults, and I am far short of perfect.[1]
—TIGER WOODS, PROFESSIONAL GOLFER, ADMITTING HIS EXTRAMARITAL AFFAIRS IN A STATEMENT RELEASED IN DECEMBER 2009, JUST DAYS AFTER HE DENIED THE ALLEGATIONS

I want you to listen to me. I'm going to say this again: I did not have sexual relations with that woman, Miss Lewinsky. I never told anybody to lie, not a single time; never. These allegations are false. And I need to go back to work for the American people. Thank you.[2]
—PRESIDENT BILL CLINTON, JANUARY 26, 1998, NINE DAYS AFTER THE MONICA LEWINSKY SCANDAL BROKE

Indeed, I did have a relationship with Ms. Lewinsky that was not appropriate. In fact, it was wrong. It constituted a critical lapse in judgment and a personal failure on my part for which I am solely and completely responsible....Now, this matter is between me, the two people I love most—my wife and our daughter—and our God. I must put it right, and I am prepared to do whatever it takes to do so.[3]
—PRESIDENT BILL CLINTON, AUGUST 17, 1998

I have sinned against you, my Lord, and I would ask that Your precious blood would wash and cleanse every stain until it is in the seas of God's forgiveness.[4]
—EVANGELIST JIMMY SWAGGART IN A TEARFUL CONFESSION AIRED FROM HIS LOUISIANA CHURCH ON FEBRUARY 21, 1988

Everyone is like a moon, and has a dark side which he never shows to anybody.[5]
—MARK TWAIN

The man who can keep a secret may be wise, but he is not half as wise as the man with no secrets to keep.[6]
—EDGAR WATSON HOWE, NOVELIST

10 LIES

Lie #8

A MAN SHOULD NEVER ADMIT HIS WEAKNESSES.

L IKE MOST NINE-YEAR-OLDS, Alan Chambers didn't know much about sex, and he didn't think about it too often. He was busy playing with his *Star Wars* action figures, watching TV, or doing math homework. And he had no idea that his boyhood innocence was about to be snatched from him by a friendly intruder.

The unexpected invasion occurred on a warm spring day in 1981 when several relatives were visiting the Chambers's home in Winter Park, Florida. The adults were conversing in the kitchen, and most of the visiting cousins were playing in the backyard when Alan went to his bedroom. Suddenly his fourteen-year-old cousin entered and closed the door.

"Take off your clothes. I want to try something," the older boy ordered. Alan had always admired his cousin. He was tall, broad-shouldered, and athletic. He was everything Alan wished he could be when he grew up. Sensing just a tinge of fear but not knowing why, Alan decided not to resist because he wanted his cousin to like him.

The next few minutes were a painful blur. Alan bent over his small twin bed looking at the blue quilted spread covered with images of

Chewbacca, Han Solo, and *Star Wars* robots. He gazed at the stuffed dog that always sat on his pillow. Alan couldn't comprehend what was happening. His heart was racing, his palms were sweating, but he didn't know if what his cousin was doing to him was good or bad. It felt uncomfortable, but he liked the fact that someone he loved was paying attention to him. His innocent mind was filled with a million questions—but he couldn't access any answers from his limited understanding of sexuality.

This is weird, he thought. *Does this mean I'm a girl? Will I get pregnant? Will I get sick?*

When the incident was over, Alan's cousin warned him sternly, "Don't say anything to anybody. They won't believe you, and you would get in trouble."

Alan agreed to keep quiet—even though he was screaming for help on the inside. He didn't realize he had been raped and that his personality had just been violently disfigured. He didn't know that his own gender identity—his sense of maleness—had been uprooted. And he didn't realize that this seemingly harmless episode on a sunny Florida afternoon would completely alter his destiny.

Alan's story of boyhood sex abuse isn't unique, but his has a much happier ending than most. Although the incident in his bedroom so many years ago led him into a homosexual lifestyle, he found emotional healing and eventual transformation in 1991 after receiving counseling from a Christian ministry in Orlando. Today he has a wife and two children and serves as president of Exodus International, the nation's largest Christian outreach to people who struggle with same-sex attraction.

"I'm healed today," Alan told me when I wrote a profile of him for *New Man* magazine. "But it didn't happen overnight. I had to get gut-level honest about my past, and then I had to find a group of Christians who would love me no matter what I had done."[7]

LIVING WITH DIRTY SECRETS

Alan's experience is more common than we would like to think. One organization, Childcare U.S.A., says 20 percent of men in the United States have been sexually abused, compared to 38 percent of women.[8] But sex abuse is only one of many secrets men hide. Although we are experts at wearing tough, macho exteriors, most men feel inwardly weak, fearful, and insecure because of their secret shame. French historian André Malraux put it this way: "What is man? A miserable little pile of secrets."[9]

We could certainly say this about Adam, the first man. What was his first inclination after sinning against God? He tried to cover up his sin by wearing fig leaves. Then he tried to hide. When God confronted him, Adam tried to shift the blame to his wife. This is how guilt operates.

Through my years of praying with men for spiritual freedom, I have learned that most guys carry one or more miserable secrets. Sometimes these are related to a traumatic memory. Other times the secret is a sinful habit or serious moral failure they have never confessed to anyone. Like the sailor in Samuel Taylor Coleridge's poem "The Rime of the Ancient Mariner" who was forced to wear a dead albatross around his neck to remind him of his sin, men often carry a heavy burden of guilt throughout life.[10]

And the longer we carry guilt, the heavier it becomes. In Charles Dickens's classic novel *A Christmas Carol*, Ebenezer Scrooge was tormented in his old age by all the mistakes of his past. When the ghost of his dead business partner, Jacob Marley, visited him on Christmas Eve, he was wearing rusty iron chains that represented his guilt for exploiting the poor. When Scrooge asked about the chains, Marley replied, "I wear the chain I forged in life. I made it link by link, and yard by yard; I girded it on of my own free will, and of my own free will I wore it."[11]

Then Marley revealed that Scrooge's chain was even longer. He said, "Or would you know the weight and length of the strong coil you bear yourself? It was full as heavy and as long as this, seven Christmas Eves ago. You have laboured on it, since. It is a ponderous chain!"[12]

Do you carry a heavy chain?

Guilt is actually a blessing, because it is designed to drive us back to God so we can find forgiveness through the blood of Christ. But if we don't turn to Him for help, we must carry the blame ourselves—and the chain grows longer and heavier over the years. This is why many men become emotionally hardened, almost like statues, as they grow older. They bury their guilt under layers of denial and deceit, then they lose complete touch with their emotions, then their consciences become seared. Eventually they become incapable of developing meaningful relationships or of showing love. Sin has destructive power!

Men hide their guilt in various ways. Some drink alcohol, smoke cigarettes, or take various substances, either prescription medicines or illegal drugs, to numb the nagging sense of condemnation. Others become workaholics, thinking that if they stay busy enough they won't have time to think about their problems; others withdraw from normal interaction with people or become obsessed with certain hobbies (like video games) or sports. In extreme cases, guilt-laden men become so angry that their bitterness erupts into abusive behavior or even criminal activity.

Confession of sin is never easy, because our stubborn pride stands in the way. But it is especially difficult for men to confess certain sins because of the cultural stigma attached to them. Sexual sins are particularly tough because many churches don't provide a climate of acceptance and unconditional love for people who admit they have struggled in these areas.

I had a friend who waged a difficult battle with pornography. When he finally worked up the nerve to talk about this problem with a man in his church, the man cut off all communication and never spoke to my friend again—and he told others that my friend could never be eligible for any form of lay leadership in the church. Needless to say, this cold, judgmental reaction made it harder for this wounded brother to make himself vulnerable again. He felt like crawling in a shell and never coming out.

That's how shame creates a vicious cycle. When a guy sins, he is afraid to expose his failures to the light of God's love because he fears rejection. So he hides his sin deeper, and this becomes a pattern. The deeper he sinks into the shame, the more fear he has of admitting his problem. Before too long, he is drowning in guilt.

There are many kinds of secrets men carry, but here's a list of the most common.

1. Trauma

Some guys have been exposed to horrible things as children or teenagers that no human being should witness. One man I know was just a child when he crawled into a bedroom closet and listened as his father severely beat his mother. Children who witness such violence often feel they are responsible for the abuse. Yet it can be difficult for men to admit ugly family secrets. Other men I know witnessed atrocities on the battlefield when they served in the military—or they actually killed people in combat. Many veterans struggle with intense feelings of guilt, and this can even lead to post-traumatic stress disorder or more serious mental problems.

2. Fornication

Our permissive culture encourages unmarried people to engage in sex before marriage. Men's magazines such as *GQ* and *Men's Health* assume that all guys engage in intercourse with multiple girlfriends, and the only rule they offer is a politically correct warning: "Be sure to wear a condom." But the truth is that God did not design us to become sexually intimate with every woman who comes along. He wants us to be joined to one wife for life. God's will, according to 1 Thessalonians 4:3, is that we "abstain from fornication" (KJV).

Fornication refers to any form of sex outside the boundaries of heterosexual marriage.

Men who were promiscuous before becoming Christians can find full forgiveness when they are converted. But professing Christians who have sex with their girlfriends or choose to cohabit with them often rationalize this behavior by saying that they are "practicing" for marriage or "making sure we are compatible." This type of spiritual compromise will produce a major load of guilt, no matter how much our culture applauds such behavior.

3. Adultery

In the 1987 film *Fatal Attraction* a successful New York lawyer, Dan Gallagher, who has a wife and young daughter, ends up having a weekend affair with a beautiful book editor named Alex.[13] He thinks the fling is a harmless, one-night stand—until Alex starts stalking him and his family, and Dan realizes she is mentally unstable. The message of the film is bold: once you commit adultery, you can't hide it. Glenn Close, the actress who played Alex, has told reporters that men often tell her that *Fatal Attraction* saved their marriage because it scared them so much.

Yet there are Christian men today who carry the guilt of an extramarital affair for years. They've never told their wives, their pastors, or a trusted friend. Like King David, who lied about his affair with Bathsheba and even had her husband killed as part of the cover-up, these men will live in perpetual suffering until they come clean.

4. Abortion

We often focus on the guilt that women feel after they kill an unborn child, and we even have a clinical term for it: post-abortion stress disorder. But men who get women pregnant and then abort the babies bear the same burden of responsibility. They are haunted by the daily reminder that the pregnancy they paid to end was in fact a human life.

5. Pornography

When I was a teenager, the only type of pornography that was accessible was soft-core material like *Playboy*. In order to obtain it, a boy had to bravely carry the magazine to a counter and buy it. Meanwhile, hard-core porn was only available in seedy downtown shops with painted windows, and those establishments strictly forbade anyone under age eighteen from entering. That's no longer the case. Today, hard-core porn of every imaginable variety is just a click away on the Internet or cable television, and kids can easily access it. Watching porn (often while masturbating) is considered part of a male college student's normal routine, and many older men today are porn addicts.

I'm convinced the proliferation of pornography is the number-one cancer eating at the soul of men around the world. Like the forbidden fruit that Adam tasted, porn is difficult to resist. The sights and sounds of it cause a heart-thumping rush of adrenaline and the thrill of sexual arousal. Once men indulge in it, porn can become as powerful an addiction as cocaine. Yet the guilt associated with pornography is one of the major reasons why Christian men live defeated spiritual lives.

6. Same-sex attraction

Of all the secrets men carry, this one is the hardest for men to admit. Even though many men entertain same-sex thoughts from time to time, and even though many of them engaged in some type of same-sex activity as children or teens (often out of sheer curiosity), few men are willing to tell anyone about this for fear of being labeled a homosexual.

Other guys have struggled with latent same-sex feelings since childhood, often because of a lack of proper fathering—or because of sexual abuse. Mainstream society tells these men to relax and embrace homosexuality as an inborn personality trait. Evangelical Christians and some in the psychiatric community disagree, maintaining that homosexuality is a form of emotional brokenness that can be reformed through prayer and counseling.

Christians who counsel men with same-sex attraction issues believe homosexuality can actually be, in some cases, an inborn trait in some males, just as some men are more prone to alcoholism, anger, or heterosexual promiscuity because of generational sins passed down from parents or grandparents. They also believe many men are drawn into the gay lifestyle because they did not have a strong father figure in the home, and their craving for male affection opened the door for gender confusion. We should have compassion for guys who struggle with their sexual identity rather than demeaning them.

The church has been sadly silent on these issues and lacking in true compassion for the homosexual community. While we cannot compromise the biblical injunction against homosexuality (as if we could change God's nature and the laws of His universe), we must be willing to reach out to men (and women) who struggle with this sin—rather than treating them like lepers. If you are a straight guy with healthy sexual values, God can use you as a big brother or father figure to help bring emotional healing to a man who struggles in his sexuality.

Whether homosexuality is a learned behavior or a generational predisposition, or a combination of both, there is no question that forgiveness and healing is available through Jesus Christ.

7. Sexual abuse

Christian men who were abused as boys are often too embarrassed to talk about their pain, either because churches don't understand sexual dysfunction or because they are downright judgmental and condemning toward those who face this issue. As a result, many men suffer in silence.

Through his work with Exodus International, Alan Chambers has learned firsthand how rampant sexual abuse is in America. He says the majority of the men who come for counseling at his Florida office were molested by a family member or friend. One survey of ex-gay men revealed that 51 percent of them were molested before age eighteen.

"A boy who has been raped by a man may develop a belief that he is somehow feminine, because a male was so powerfully attracted to him," says David Kyle Foster, a counselor based in Nashville, Tennessee, and author of the book *Sexual Healing*.[14] "The boy may grow up with the incident of abuse obsessively fixed in his mind. Somehow the mind of a child can become scrambled, and he thinks that he is somehow meant for the sexual satisfaction of his own gender."

8. Other forms of perversion

Men can be haunted by all kinds of dirty secrets, ranging from incest to public exhibitionism to bestiality to an obsession with women's underwear. Sometimes the enemy of our souls lures men into perverse experiences so that he can torment them with guilt and, in essence, claim their souls. Shameful memories become like monkeys on our backs, following us everywhere.

Many young people today are also being tempted to engage in sexual practices that are mixed with occult spirituality. I know of one young man who got caught up in the bizarre, underground vampire subculture in which youth drink each other's blood. These practices are sometimes associated with the dark Goth culture. These kinds of experiences not only bring heavy guilt but also open the human soul to serious demonic oppression.

9. Masturbation

While the Bible does not directly label masturbation a sin, it does list "impurity" as a work of the flesh in Galatians 5:19. (The Contemporary English Version translates this word as "filthy thoughts.") Because masturbation is often accompanied by the viewing of pornography and/or immoral fantasies, men who engage in this behavior also struggle with severe guilt.

In the church today, there are differing opinions about whether masturbation should be condemned. Some evangelical leaders teach that it's OK for younger guys, since it provides a sexual release at a time when their sex drive is most active. (They suggest that single men who masturbate before a date might not be as tempted to engage in premarital sex.) Others take a stricter approach, saying that all masturbation is a form of impurity, especially since sexual arousal usually requires fantasies.

My view is that a man who wants to walk in holiness before God must live with a clean conscience. If masturbation brings the uncomfortable heaviness of a guilty conscience, then he should avoid it. And if a man is married, he must recognize that when he masturbates, he is robbing his wife of the sexual pleasure he owes her. A man who focuses his sexual energy on himself is never going to have an intimate relationship with his wife.

10. Domestic abuse

Severe guilt will hang over any man who harms his wife or children. This applies to physical, emotional, and sexual abuse. In fact, the man who mistreats his wife will actually feel cut off from fellowship with God. The apostle Peter wrote:

> You husbands in the same way, live with your wives in an understanding way, as with someone weaker, since she is a woman; and show her honor as a fellow heir of the grace of life, *so that your prayers will not be hindered.*
> —1 PETER 3:7, EMPHASIS ADDED

According to this passage, a man who devalues his wife by screaming at her, hitting her, or abusing her in any way forfeits communication with God altogether. His connection to God cannot be restored until he swallows his pride, confesses his sin, and adjusts his attitude.

11. Dishonesty and other unethical behavior

History is littered with accounts of powerful men who tried to deny their wrongdoing when they got caught. President Richard Nixon made his famous "I am not a crook" speech in 1973, but he resigned from office the next year after tape recordings revealed that he knew about the Watergate cover-up and had tried to stop an FBI investigation. He never actually admitted to any wrongdoing.

Many men today live with skeletons in their office closets. They may have lied to a client to close a sale, passed a bribe, used unethical accounting practices, or done something illegal on the job. In the world of professional sports, some men use illegal drugs to gain a physical advantage; in the end, any temporary victory they win turns sour. Cheating will never get you ahead in the long run. This is where we need to apply the sobering words of Moses in Numbers 32:23: "Behold, you have sinned against the LORD, and be sure your sin will find you out."

12. Neglect

I once met a traveling evangelist who claimed to have a powerful national ministry. Yet I later learned that he was wanted by the police in a western state because he owed back child support to a former wife. I could not understand how this man had the audacity to stand in a pulpit when he had so much unfinished business at home. How could he even sleep at night, knowing that he had fathered children yet was not providing for them? The apostle Paul tells us that a man who is not a faithful steward of his own family has no business representing God in the ministry (1 Tim. 3:5).

Likewise, any man who runs from the responsibility of caring for his wife or children will live under a cloud of guilt until he stops being a deadbeat dad. A real man will admit his wrong and pay whatever amount is necessary to provide for his family's needs.

Let's Talk About It

1. Men have a natural tendency to hide their sin. How did the first man, Adam, respond after he sinned against God?
2. How does God use guilt in our lives to draw us back to Him?
3. Has there ever been a time in your life when you hid a secret sin and then finally admitted it? Can you talk about this openly?
4. Why are sexual sins especially difficult to talk about in a Christian environment?

YOU NEED TO SPILL YOUR GUTS

So many Christian men today are trapped in one or more of the sins I've listed in this chapter. They feel defeated, unworthy, and disqualified, but they suffer in silence. Their consciences remind them of their shameful secrets every day. But all they know to do is pretend that things are fine. Life becomes an act. They get up every day, put on their business suits or their work uniforms, and shuffle through life hoping that no one ever finds out who they really are.

This is not the way God intended us to live. This is not the "abundant life" that Jesus promised us in John 10:10. He came to forgive us our sins, wash us from the stains of the past, and free us from chains of guilt. Christ's death on the cross fully paid for all of our secrets.

But in order for us to fully appropriate all the blessings of salvation, we must fully recognize our need for cleansing. And this requires exposure. We must bring our secret sins into the light of His holiness to He can set us free from sin's power.

Baptist pastor Jerry Sutton, author of *A Simple Guide to the Way Back Home*, says we really only have two choices when it comes to dealing with our secrets:

When it comes to sins, we can deal with them one of two ways. We can cover them, which means deal with them our way. Or, we can confess and forsake them, which is dealing with them God's way. People cover sins by rationalizing them, by calling them a habit, by compartmentalizing their minds and ignoring that compartment, by excusing them, by blaming someone else for them, or even by procrastinating— "I will deal with them...tomorrow." Those ways of dealing with sins simply prolong the estrangement.[15]

The apostle John said it this way in 1 John 1:7–9:

> But if we walk in the Light as He Himself is in the Light, we have fellowship with one another, and the blood of Jesus His Son cleanses us from all sin. If we say that we have no sin, we are deceiving ourselves and the truth is not in us. If we confess our sins, He is faithful and righteous to forgive us our sins and to cleanse us from all unrighteousness.

Freedom requires real honesty. If you can't talk openly with someone about your sinful habits or struggles, you will never walk in the full realm of forgiveness that is available to you. I encourage you to take these five steps as soon as possible:

1. Find a brother you can trust.

You can't just talk to anybody. Your best bet is to identify a mature Christian man who has a solid walk with God. Your pastor would be an ideal choice, if you feel comfortable talking with him. Or it could be another pastor on your church's staff, or a close friend who knows you well. Make an appointment with this man and tell him you need to share something very personal. Try to meet in a private place where no one can overhear your conversation.

2. Open your heart and talk honestly about your secret.

Begin by asking your friend to keep the conversation private. If he cares about your friendship, he will assure you of total confidentiality. Then tell him that you have been tormented by guilt associated with whatever past sins are haunting you. Don't beat around the bush or minimize anything. Be a man and come clean.

Some guys find this extremely difficult. Their palms sweat, their knees knock, and their hearts race. Some guys will begin to cry, even if they have never allowed themselves to cry before. That's OK. Let the tears flow. Confession is good for the soul, and weeping is God's way of giving you an emotional release from all the shame you have buried for so long.

After confessing their sin, some men automatically expect to be rejected or shunned. We imagine that our friend will look at us with disgust and shout, "You did *what*?" That is not going to happen. A godly Christian brother will embrace you, comfort you, and accept you. He might even share some of his own failures as a reminder that all men struggle with sin. Don't let fear of rejection stop you from obeying the biblical step of confession.

3. Receive healing prayer.

James 5:16 says, "Therefore, confess your sins to one another, and pray for one another so that you may be healed. The effective prayer of a righteous man can accomplish much." Confession is only a first step. We need specific prayer for healing and closure.

This may not all happen in one session. In fact, after you meet with your friend you may realize that you need regular counseling in some area. Your friend can help you find the right environment for you to receive all the help you need. Men who were sexually abused as boys, for example, may also need deliverance from demonic powers. A man who has been battering his wife will need ongoing counseling (as will his spouse).

Men who struggle with same-sex attraction can find help from

Exodus International or another similar ex-gay ministry. Groups like this provide specialized resources tailored to this problem. When Alan Chambers, the founder of Exodus, joined an accountability group, his heterosexual friend Kirk offered counsel, prayer, and nonsexual hugs. The affection, which caused Alan to weep for five hours straight on one occasion, helped him regain his sexual identity. Kirk's hugs, in a sense, filled the void left by Alan's unaffectionate dad.

4. Make yourself accountable.

After you have made your confession and receive prayer, you may also need to join a regular support group that is tailored to your needs. Many churches today offer classes for men who have been addicted to pornography.

Some men will also need to make restitution for their sins. If a man confesses to stealing property from his employer or lying about his income taxes, he will need to pay back the money he stole. A man who has been trapped in an extramarital affair must be held accountable to end the relationship and work to restore his marriage.

5. Face your pain and forgive.

If you were sexually abused, try to contact the person who abused you and then confront them. Before you speak with the person, however, you must forgive them from your heart and seek to have Christ's compassion for them. Don't approach them if you still have anger or bitterness in your heart.

Today many men who have never had the courage to face the pain of abuse are seeking help from Christian counselors. One of them is Jim Bakker, the former televangelist, who admitted in his book *I Was Wrong* that he was sexually abused at age eleven by a young man in his church.[16] Bakker told *Charisma* magazine that it wasn't until he went to prison that he came to terms with the abuse and talked about it with a prison chaplain.[17]

"I spent my lifetime thinking the abuse was my fault," Bakker said.

"The first time I shared my story at a men's meeting in a Florida church, I was shocked by the number of men who came up to me and told me they too had been molested as children."[18]

The lie says men should never admit their weaknesses. But the truth is that only men who are vulnerable and honest will find true strength of character. Male pride is actually the greatest enemy of true manhood.

Let's Talk About It

1. James 5:16 says we should confess our sins to one another. Why is it so important for us to talk to another person about our deepest secrets? Isn't it enough to tell God?
2. What is usually the greatest barrier to confessing our sins to someone else?
3. What is restitution, and why is it so important? Give an example of a sin that might require restitution.
4. After reading this chapter, do you feel you need to make an appointment with another brother and confess something? Are you willing to commit to doing that?

THE MONSTER IN YOUR BASEMENT

When I was a kid I was terrified of the gilled fish-man who attacked scientists on a boat in *The Creature From the Black Lagoon*. I also had a few nightmares after watching those silly *Godzilla* movies, and I was terrified of the evil flying monkeys in *The Wizard of Oz*. When I got older I got a few fun scares from the astronaut-eating monster in *Alien* and the three-thousand-year-old walking corpse in *The Mummy Returns*.

I can joke about movie monsters since they aren't real. I can even laugh and eat popcorn while I watch revitalized dinosaurs chasing people in *Jurassic Park*. But if I am honest, I have to admit that I face a different kind of monster every day. It is the monster of my sin nature. And it is no laughing matter.

All of us are familiar with this monster. The apostle Paul, writing to the Romans, said sin always has a pull on us. Romans 7:18–21 says:

> For I know that nothing good dwells in me, that is, in my flesh; for the willing is present in me, but the doing of the good is not. For the good that I want, I do not do, but I practice the very evil that I do not want. But if I am doing the very thing I do not want, I am no longer the one doing it, but sin which dwells in me. I find then the principle that evil is present in me, the one who wants to do good.

I am sure you relate to Paul's honest words. He is not talking about the struggle of a person before conversion. He is describing our journey of faith after we give our hearts to Christ. Even though the Holy Spirit lives in us, we have a battle on our hands. Our sin nature constantly rages. Our flesh wants to disobey the law of God even though our awakened conscience wants to do what is right. We all face this conflict.

Over the years I have counseled many young men who face daily sexual temptations. Often these guys come to me discouraged and frustrated. They love God, and they try to serve Him faithfully, but they feel overwhelmed by the pull of sin. Pornography is easily accessible on their computers, and some of their friends are living in immoral relationships. So these guys ask me how they can live pure lives in a sex-saturated culture.

I always turn to Romans 7 and remind my friends that the apostle Paul, probably the greatest Christian who ever lived, shared their struggle. We don't know if sexual temptation was a major problem for him, but he admitted that he felt weak when he faced the attraction of sin.

I have often used this passage in Romans as the basis for an analogy about a monster in my basement. I will share it with you.

Suppose you live in a two-story house with a basement. You rarely go down into the lowest level of the house because you know there is a caged monster down there. You can hear it growling every day, and you know it is bloodthirsty. It has fangs, claws, and a hideous appearance.

But it cannot bite you because it is locked in a cage. All it can do is scare you—unless, of course, you decide to venture into the basement and stick your hand between the bars. Or if you want to be even more stupid, you can take the key hanging on the wall, open the cage, and give it some food.

The best option would be to ignore the monster. And it would be easier to ignore its growling if you spent most of your time on the top floor of the house—as far away from the noise as possible. The monster would still be there, but if you are so far above it that you can't hear its menacing cries, you will never go near it.

This is essentially what Paul told the Romans to do with their sin nature. First he asked an obvious question: "Wretched man that I am! Who will set me free from the body of this death?" (Rom. 7:24). Then he provided the answer:

> Thanks be to God through Jesus Christ our Lord! So then, on the one hand I myself with my mind am serving the law of God, but on the other, with my flesh the law of sin. Therefore there is now no condemnation for those who are in Christ Jesus. For the law of the Spirit of life in Christ Jesus has set you free from the law of sin and of death.
>
> —ROMANS 7:25–8:2

Paul calls us higher, to a place of escape. Although we will never be completely free from the pull of sin in this life, God gives us, through the covenant of grace, a means to drown out the sound of the monster in our basement. It is grace that seats us in heavenly places with Christ so that we are no longer on the same level with sin; we can live above it. Just as the law of aerodynamics lifts a plane above the ground and supersedes the law of gravity, so the law of the Spirit of life in Christ Jesus lifts us above temptation and the bondage of sin.

If you are struggling with a sinful habit or a constant temptation, or if you have fallen into sin multiple times and feel like a failure, leave the basement and climb to the top level of your house. Shut the door on the chained monster and rise above it. Take your position with the resurrected Christ, who has risen above sin and become its master.

And as you plant your feet firmly above the monster of your sin nature, meditate on the truth of Paul's words in Romans 6:14: "For sin shall not be master over you, for you are not under law but under grace." Christ lives in you, and His grace has been freely given to empower you in this conflict. You can look down on the raging monster of sin and tell it to be quiet.

Let's Pray About It

Father, I don't want anything to hinder my relationship with You. I lay my heart bare before You. Strip me of any pride that has deceitfully covered my sin. Help me to be honest with You about the condition of my heart. Help me to swallow my fears of exposure so that I can bring all my failures and weaknesses into Your light. Amen.

I do not weep: I loathe tears, for they are a sign of slavery.[1]
—MAX BECKMANN

---

*I often want to cry. That is the only advantage
women have over men—at least they can cry.*[2]
—JEAN RHYS

---

*Laughter and tears are both responses to frustra-
tion and exhaustion. . . . I myself prefer to laugh, since
there is less cleaning up to do afterward.*[3]
—KURT VONNEGUT, AUTHOR

Tears are God's gift to us. Our holy water. They heal us as they flow.[4]
—RITA SCHIANO

Tearless grief bleeds inwardly.[5]
—CHRISTIAN NEVELL BOVEE

What soap is for the body, tears are for the soul.[6]
—JEWISH PROVERB

---

*Tears shed for self are tears of weakness, but tears
shed for others are a sign of strength.*[7]
—EVANGELIST BILLY GRAHAM

---

10 LIES

Lie #9

REAL MEN DON'T CRY.

I'VE NEVER MET George Banks. That would be impossible, since he is the fictional dad played by Steve Martin in the 1991 film *Father of the Bride*.[8] But I feel I know George because I've watched the sappy comedy so many times. I watched it again just before my second daughter's wedding in late 2009.

I guess the film provides a mild form of therapy. It helps me deal with my loss. Despite what they all say—"You're not losing a daughter! You're gaining a son!"—I started to feel an uncomfortable lump in my throat at least seventy-two hours before the ceremony. Yes, I knew that I, a grown man, would cry at this wedding. When my oldest daughter, Margaret, married in 2008, my tears started flowing as soon as the grandmothers were seated. I wondered, Would I keep it together this time?

Giving away a daughter is a huge deal for a dad. While I am not as high-strung as George Banks, I identify with his paternal anxieties. Like most fathers, he worried that his daughter's fiancé might be a criminal in disguise; he also fretted about the boyfriend's rich parents (and snooped around in their desk drawers to find out how much money they made); and, in almost every scene, he hyperventilated about the costs of the wedding cake, the tuxedos, and the food for the reception.

While most people just laugh at George, I empathize. I knew how much the wedding would cost when I added up the church rental fee, the caterer's fee, the photographer's fee, the florist's fee, the musicians' fee, and the cost of the wedding gown. I understood why George wanted to have the reception at his favorite restaurant, The Steak Pit. (His son's advice: "Dad, I don't think you want the word *pit* on a wedding invitation.")

In the movie, George's pent-up wedding anxiety erupted in a fit of anger over the cost of hot dog buns—and he landed in jail after he threatened a grocery store manager in the bread aisle.

I never assaulted anyone during my first or second daughters' engagements. I decided to trust God to provide for all the wedding expenses. But that is much easier than trusting the guy who is standing at the church altar with the ear-to-ear grin. He's taking your little girl on a honeymoon and then living with her for the rest of her life—and supporting her on...what?

All fathers of daughters must face this inevitable moment. I knew someday a groom would replace me. I had to let go.

I knew from memory the words that would be read from Genesis 2:24 in the ceremony: "For this reason a man shall leave his father and his mother, and be joined to his wife; and they shall be one flesh." That verse sounded so romantic at my own wedding; now it sounded cold, ominous, and very, very final.

When Georgia Meredith came up the stairs from the church basement that cool December evening and grabbed my arm, twenty-two years of memories flooded my brain in a second. This was the little girl who, at age three, broke her tooth when she fell off her tricycle. This is the girl who loved to read animal encyclopedias with her dad after everyone else in the family had gone to sleep.

Now she was wearing a flowing gown and looking like a princess, only I was not her Prince Charming. My job was simply to escort her down the aisle and place her hand in his.

I managed the tears OK at first. They didn't flow in full force. When the pastor asked, "Who gives this woman to marry this man?" I coughed up my one official line, "Her mother and I," and grabbed enough breath to whisper to Sven, "She's all yours."

But when Sven started repeating his vows to Meredith, he choked up. That set off a chain reaction, and I lost it. Within a few seconds both the groom and the father of the bride were a mess. I didn't recover until the couple exchanged rings.

In *Father of the Bride*, George didn't get to talk to his daughter at the reception because he was too busy moving cars that were illegally parked in front of his house. We did not have any parking problems at Meredith and Sven's wedding. I was able to say the proper good-byes to Meredith, and we danced together to Ray Charles's "Georgia on My Mind."

I let go of my little girl, but the tears flowed a few more times after the wedding. And my eyes still mist up slightly when I hear that song.

THE DREADED "SISSY" WORD

I actually found it easy to cry at my daughter's wedding. After all, I was fifty-one years old—and I really didn't care what anyone thought. But it was not always that way. When I was younger, I was conditioned by my culture to believe that men should never cry.

This became painfully real to me when I was about nine years old. Every August my parents took my sister and me to a family reunion in east Alabama. I looked forward to those days mainly because I loved to play with my younger cousin, Chris, in a huge community swimming pool. There was so much love and family togetherness during those three days that I hated it to end. When lunch was over the last day and the kids were told to get out of the pool, I began to cry. I simply did not want to leave all my aunts, uncles, and cousins.

I'll never forget the sense of embarrassment and shame that I felt as I sniffled in the backseat of our family sedan. My parents probably just thought I was being childish. I was especially embarrassed that I was crying in front of my older sister. And I could hear all kinds of cruel names thrown at me by imaginary voices, some of whom had said similar words to me in my third-grade classroom: "Sissy!" "Cry-baby!" or "You're such a pansy!"

Any boy who has ever been called "sissy" by his young classmates knows that those words can cut like a knife and lodge inside your soul like a festering splinter. To question a boy's maleness at that young age is traumatic, and such mean-spirited labeling can cause deep insecurity, gender confusion, or deep-seated anxiety. In my case, I feared that word so much that I built a protective wall around my heart. I swallowed hard and vowed that I would never cry again. I had to act tough. I had to pretend that I was strong.

I went through my teenage years wearing an invisible force field of protection. I did everything possible to avoid a sign of weakness. I never wanted to be called a sissy again—so I bottled up my emotions, kept my eyes dry, and avoided the class bullies who just might pull that dreaded word out of their verbal arsenal. My greatest fear in life was to have my manhood challenged—especially in front of a group of giggling preteen boys.

But there was one problem: I did not really understand what real manhood was all about. Those bullies didn't either. They were just as insecure as I was (maybe even more so)—and they called other boys sissies because they doubted their own masculinity.

My deliverance came at age eighteen when I surrendered my life to Jesus and asked Him to be the Lord of my life. As I began to study God's Word, I discovered that men in the Bible did not stifle their emotions. In fact, it seemed that Bible characters lived in a totally different world than my own. In both the Old and New Testament times, the most masculine heroes were emotionally free.

Esau, who would definitely fit the description of a macho man (he was a hairy guy who loved to hunt), wept profusely when he was reconciled with his twin brother, Jacob (Gen. 33:4).

Joseph wept so loudly when he was reunited with his estranged brothers that everyone in Pharaoh's house heard his sobbing (Gen. 45:2).

King David, who defeated Goliath and led his armies into battle, cried often. His tears flowed freely in worship (Ps. 39:12), and he didn't hide his tears when his wives and children were kidnapped in a raid at Ziklag (1 Sam. 30:4). And when he realized that he must flee from Saul and leave his covenant friend Jonathan, the two men wept together (1 Sam. 20:41).

King Hezekiah wept in remorse as he prayed for healing (2 Kings 20:3), while God honored King Josiah because of his tears of repentance (2 Kings 22:19).

Nehemiah wept in intercession for the ruined city of Jerusalem (Neh. 1:4), and his emotional display released the king's favor on his mission to rebuild.

And we cannot forget Jeremiah, the man known as "the weeping prophet." He declared in Jeremiah 9:1, "Oh that my head were waters and my eyes a fountain of tears, that I might weep day and night for the slain of the daughter of my people!"

When we come to the New Testament, we see that Jesus Himself was completely comfortable shedding tears in public. He wept when His friend Lazarus died, causing the mourners to notice the depth of His love (John 11:35), and He wept over the city of Jerusalem because He knew the fate of those who would perish there (Luke 19:41). The writer of Hebrews also tells us that Jesus obtained our salvation through "loud crying and tears" when He surrendered to God's will in the garden of Gethsemane (Heb. 5:7).

Finally, the apostle Paul literally spilled tears on his epistles because of his love for the early church. He said he "wrote to you with many tears" (2 Cor. 2:4), he wept as he admonished the Ephesians (Acts 20:31), and he often spoke of deep, travailing intercession—the kind of prayer that involves "groanings too deep for words" (Rom. 8:26).

If all these men—including the Son of God Himself—could find such freedom to weep without shame or regret, why is it so hard for us today to be emotionally vulnerable? Could it be that the enemy of our souls has engineered a conspiracy to keep men in a prison of fear that prevents them from releasing godly emotions? I believe this is exactly Satan's tactic.

THE FORGOTTEN POWER OF BROKENNESS

After I surrendered to the lordship of Christ, I was soon filled with the Holy Spirit. This helped me to gain new revelation from the Bible, and I began to discover the Father's love for me. I also began to figure out who I really was and how God made me.

I learned that He created me to be an emotional creature. I had tear ducts for a reason. I also discovered that He gave me a sensitive nature. I cried easily, not because I was weak or effeminate but because He had given me the kind of prophetic personality that empathizes with other people's pain and discerns the spiritual realm.

After I was filled with the Holy Spirit, I began to experience the healing of my damaged emotions. This is a process of renewal that is available to every Christian. I stopped believing the lies that I had believed about myself. I let go of all unforgiveness and resentment that I had in my heart toward people who had hurt me. I even found emotional freedom from the pain caused by those hurtful words that had been thrown at me when I was a child. This process of inner healing is described this way in Ezekiel 36:26 (emphasis added):

> Moreover, I will give you a new heart and put a new spirit within you; *and I will remove the heart of stone from your flesh* and give you a heart of flesh.

Notice that God says He will remove the "heart of stone." This is what many men today struggle to overcome. Our hearts are hardened by sin, by wrong choices, by pride, and by our stubborn refusal to listen to God's instructions. When we come to the Lord, He provides His Holy Spirit to complete the softening process so that we can hear the Lord's voice, receive revelation from His Word, flow in His anointing, and effectively minister to people.

But in order for us to become useful vessels of His Spirit, we must allow God to break our "outward man," which consists of our mind, will, and emotions. If our soulish nature remains hard, God cannot flow through us.

Watchman Nee, the famous Chinese revivalist and Bible teacher who lived from 1903 to 1972, explains this important principle in his classic book *Release of the Spirit*.[9] He writes:

> No life manifests more beauty than the one who is broken! Stubbornness and self-love have given way to beauty in the one who has been broken by God.... Our only hope is that the Lord may blaze a way out of us, breaking our outward man—breaking it to such a degree that the inward man may come out and be seen. This is precious! This is the way for those who serve the Lord. Only by this process may we serve the Lord, and only by this procedure can we lead men to the Lord.... Only the person through whom God can come forth is useful.[10]

Nee taught that God uses various trials and difficulties in our lives to break the outward man. God wants to pulverize all the hardness in our hearts; He wants us to be like soft, moldable putty in His hands. While He certainly has called us as men to be strong in the Lord "and in the strength of His might" (Eph. 6:10), He does not want us to be hard, tough, stubborn, or prideful. We must surrender all hardness to Him.

There really is nothing more beautiful than a man who has been crushed by the holy process of God. We can see this in the example of Jacob in the Old Testament. When we first see Jacob, he is a conniving deceiver; as he grows older, he tries to manipulate circumstances to get his way. God has to bring all kinds of trials and uncomfortable circumstances into his path to crush his self-centeredness.

But in the end, we see Jacob wrestling with the angel of the Lord until daybreak. The Bible says that God touched the socket of Jacob's thigh and dislocated his hip (Gen. 32:25). Another translation says God shrunk the muscle in his thigh—which happens to be the largest muscle in the body. As the story concludes, we see Jacob walking with a noticeable limp into the sunrise. He carried that limp for the rest of his life.

If we truly desire to be men of God, we too must enter a wrestling match with God and allow Him to pin us to the ground. We must give Him permission to strike us in the place of our greatest human strength. And we must let Him crush our hard hearts and injure our pride to the point that we will forever walk with a limp.

It is precious in the sight of God when a strong man gives God permission to crush Him and make him meek, humble, and spiritually sensitive. You do not have to be afraid of this process. The crushing of God does not make you a sissy or a wimp; His power is perfected in weakness. You will win more souls, cast out more devils, and influence more people for Christ in your weakened state than you ever could as a strong, self-confident, and unbroken man.

Let's Talk About It

1. Did you grow up believing that it was not appropriate for boys to cry? Do you find it easy to cry today?
2. Why do you think men in our culture today are not as comfortable showing their emotions as men during Bible times?

3. Why is it important for every man to go through the process of spiritual brokenness?

RECOVERING OUR LOST MASCULINE EMOTIONS

Many guys have the mistaken notion that it is a woman's job to show emotions, while men should be rigid and stoic. There is absolutely nothing biblical about that philosophy. In fact stoicism, which promotes reason above any emotional display, is a pagan concept invented by the Greek philosopher Zeno.

God made both men and women as emotional creatures, and our emotions are actually reflections of the divine nature. God has the capacity to feel joy, sadness, anger, jealousy, and intense zeal. He created us with those same emotions. There is absolutely nothing in Scripture that indicates that women are more emotional or that they feel certain emotions stronger than men do.

But because of macho attitudes, insecurity, and male pride, the church has been robbed of a dynamic force because men's emotions have been bottled up and imprisoned. It is almost as if several cylinders in the church's spiritual engine were removed—making us weak and powerless. I believe Christian men must recover three lost expressions of masculine spirituality.

1. Protective compassion

My friend Randy Landis, a pastor from Pennsylvania, was one of the first Christian missionaries to fly to the nation of Haiti after a powerful earthquake struck the nation in 2010. He ventured there with four men from his church to make sure an orphanage they sponsored near Port-au-Prince was structurally sound. When Randy and his buddies arrived at the compound, they moved the children to another facility and stayed there for several days to help distribute relief supplies to quake victims.

When I talked to Randy after he returned from his trip, he broke into tears several times as he described the devastation and the effect the disaster had on the children he was responsible for. Randy is not a weak man; he's a serious golfer and a bold preacher. But seeing desperate human needs unlocked a wellspring of authentic concern in this man—and he cried freely. I respected him even more when I saw this display of tenderness.

The British revivalist George Whitefield was said to be so fervent in his preaching that he rarely made it through a sermon without tears. His friend Mr. Winter wrote of Whitefield, "Sometimes he exceedingly wept, and was frequently so overcome, that for a few seconds you would suspect that he never would recover....I hardly ever knew him to go through a sermon without weeping more or less."[11]

Whitefield once told one of his audiences, "You blame me for weeping; but how can I help it, when you will not weep for yourselves, although your own immortal souls are on the verge of destruction, and, for aught I know, you are hearing your last sermon, and may never have an opportunity to have Christ offered to you?"[12]

There is nothing more Christlike than to see a strong, masculine man crying when he feels the love of God for people. The world needs to see this kind of emotional display. Our Christianity today is way too dry. We assume we will win the world with nice spiritual words and eloquent sermons. But those words actually fall flat, even though our doctrine is perfect; they are devoid of any real emotion. We need to ask God to break our hearts so real tears can flow.

2. Holy zeal

Charles Spurgeon, the great British preacher of the 1800s, trained hundreds of ministers in his Bible school. He taught them the Word, to be sure, but he also urged them to go beyond head knowledge. Christianity is not authentic if it does not flow from the heart.

He told his students, "Ministerial success is traceable almost entirely to an intense zeal, a consuming passion for souls, and an eager enthusiasm for the cause of God, and we believe that in every case, other things being equal, men prosper in the divine service in proportion as their hearts are blazing with holy love."[13]

Spurgeon continued, "A pillar of light and fire should be the preacher's fit emblem. Our ministry must be emphatic, or it will never affect these thoughtless times; and to this end our hearts must be habitually fervent, and our whole nature must be fired with an all-consuming passion for the glory of God and the good of men."[14]

This kind of zeal is rare in American pulpits today. Often we hear half-baked, warmed-over platitudes delivered in monotone. Or, on the other extreme, we hear shouting and screaming from the pulpit, but it seems fake and contrived. In either case, it is because the men delivering the message have not been struck at the core of their being by the lightning of God.

We desperately need a baptism of fire that will translate into authentic zeal. Too many men of God today are passive and reserved about their faith. Jesus told us not to hide our light under a basket, yet we do more than hide it—we snuff it out. It is time for us to emerge like Gideon's three hundred warriors; we must break our clay pots, pull out our flaming torches, and rush to the battle line with a hot spiritual passion.

3. Fervent prayer

Nothing has been more damaging to the church than the idea that only women are called to pray. Not only has this limited our women into one narrow role (especially those who are called to serve in other ministry functions, such as teaching or preaching), but it has also kept men out of the prayer room. In most American churches, if you call a prayer meeting you will normally get about 90 percent women and 10 percent men. Most Christian men view prayer as women's work.

That is an abominable deception that has no basis in Scripture. Of course, there are plenty of women prayer warriors in the Bible. But ever since the father of our faith, Abraham, interceded on behalf of his nephew Lot in order to pull him out of the clutches of Sodom's compromise, men of God have prayed fire down from heaven, stopped the sun in its course, released heavenly armies, exposed genocide plots, and shut the mouths of lions through their prayers. For every Hannah and Deborah in the Bible we have a Daniel and an Ezekiel.

God actually wants His men to become lions in prayer. We should not be afraid to let our voices be heard. Something powerful happens when men pray, but something even more powerful happens when men enter the place of travail. Though we as men will never know the pain of childbirth, God gives us the opportunity to birth spiritual things through the groans of deep intercession.

Some men are daring enough to climb mountains or go on African safaris, but few men will dare to venture into the unknown territory of travailing prayer. Maybe because they think it is women's work, they are afraid of being called a sissy. Meanwhile the earth itself is groaning as it waits for God's mature sons to pray with genuine authority and heartfelt emotion.

After Elijah boldly confronted the prophets of Baal on Mount Carmel, the Bible says the prophet climbed to the top of the mountain, crouched down on the ground, and put his head between his knees (1 Kings 18:42). This was no ordinary prayer; it was the closest thing to childbirth Elijah would ever experience. But he did not avoid the task. He groaned in that place while his servant went to look at the sky seven times. Finally a cloud appeared "as small as a man's hand" (v. 44), but eventually the sky became black with clouds and the rain returned—all in response to a man's powerful petition.

Elijah's prayer struck fear into Ahab's heart and sent Jezebel on one last rampage. In the end, both enemies were defeated. I believe we will see similar results today when we as men break out of our emotional straitjackets and begin to pray, preach, and love people like real men.

Let's Pray About It

Father, please open up every clogged channel in my heart and release my emotions. I want to cry Your tears. Forgive me if I have been complacent, lukewarm, or passive in my spiritual devotion. I want to exhibit protective compassion, holy zeal, and fervent prayer, in Jesus's name. Amen.

And do you not know that you [women] are (each) an Eve? The sentence of God on this sex of yours lives in this age: the guilt must of necessity live too. You are the devil's gateway: you are the unsealer of that (forbidden) tree: you are the first deserter of the divine law.[1]

—TERTULLIAN

It is not proper for a woman to speak in church, however admirable or holy what she says may be, merely because it comes from female lips.[2]

—ORIGEN

Did God ever send women to preach? No, God never sent a woman to preach. Any woman that says God sent her to preach is a liar and deceived by the devil. And anyone who believes God sent a woman to preach is deceived of the devil.[3]

—BISHOP V. BUSH

Church of the Lord Jesus Christ of the Apostolic Faith: "Women preachers are a 'cancer' to Christianity and are not part of the Kingdom of God."[4]

—CALVINIST PREACHER AYMON DE ALBATRUS

---

10 LIES

A MAN SHOULD NEVER RECEIVE SPIRITUAL MINISTRY FROM A WOMAN.

ROMINENT BIBLE TEACHER Anne Graham Lotz commands respect. It's obvious when she preaches that she is the daughter of evangelist Billy Graham. Many people believe she carries her father's spiritual mantle.

But back in the 1980s, Lotz did not get the respect due her when she spoke at a conference sponsored by her denomination, the Southern Baptist Convention. When it came time for her to preach, she approached the platform and opened her Bible. Then a loud commotion began in the front of the auditorium. Lotz looked down to see that several rows of men, all dressed in dark suits, were quickly turning their chairs around.[5]

Within a few minutes it became obvious what was happening. These men, all pastors, had turned their backs to this woman to protest her inclusion in the conference schedule. They were making a bold statement, albeit a rude one. In their view, it is wrong for women to teach the Bible to men, so in their flamboyantly discourteous manner they refused to face her as she spoke. They wouldn't allow themselves to hear this woman preacher's voice, even though she was Billy Graham's daughter and even though she had something profoundly spiritual to say; to them, this was just as dangerous as listening to the mythological Sirens, who lured ancient Greek sailors to their deaths on the rocky Mediterranean coast.

I heard Lotz speak at First Baptist Church in Orlando, Florida, a few years ago. The auditorium was packed with mostly male ministers and a few of their wives. Her sermon, delivered in her trademark North Carolina drawl, made me feel welcome. Her delivery style and cadence were eerily similar to her famous father's, yet she delivered it in a totally feminine manner. She called the people in the congregation that evening to repentance and a deeper relationship with Christ. When the service was over, most people would have agreed, I am sure, that Lotz had outpreached most of the men who had stood in that same podium that week.

I was just grateful that no preachers staged a protest outside or stood up in the meeting and turned their chairs backward to protest the fact that a woman was speaking. Yet listening to Lotz reminded me that many women who are gifted speakers, teachers, and spiritual leaders don't have her famous name to open doors for them. Because of religious traditions and narrow and erroneous interpretations of Scripture, many men have developed the view that they can never receive anything spiritual from a woman.

WE NEED FATHERS *AND* MOTHERS

We all know it takes a man and a woman to create a baby. And family counselors will agree that children are best developed in a loving home that has both a mother and a father. While single parents can certainly find special grace from God to lead their families alone, God's original design has always been a two-parent family that is led by a male and a female.

Most conservative Christians would wholeheartedly agree with this arrangement, yet in their churches you will often find a strong bias against women having any public influence. Because these churches emphasize two passages of Scriptures in the New Testament that appear on the surface to limit women's ministry (1 Tim. 2:12 and 1 Cor. 14:34–35), they throw out the many other Scriptures that empower women. Then they build a rigid doctrine that forbids women to preach the gospel, lead ministries, or teach in churches.

As a result, they create a rather strange dichotomy. While they praise mothers in the natural, they leave no room for spiritual mothers in the church. They honor mothers for having babies and for fulfilling their wifely duties, but they ignore women who are gifted to bring souls into the kingdom of God.

I always found this concept odd, because God used women in my life from a young age. I came to faith as a child partly through the influence of Sunday school teachers. When I was eighteen, a woman who taught my Sunday morning college class led me into a deeper Christian experience. When I was in college, I listened to recorded teachings by a woman named Joy Dawson, a New Zealander who helped establish the Youth With A Mission organization. And when I got married and had a family, a Pentecostal preacher named Barbara James prayed for me, encouraged me, and opened ministry doors for me. She became like a spiritual mother. I still treasure her in that role today.

The Book of Proverbs touches on this vital truth. Solomon tells his son in Proverbs 1:8–9:

> Hear, my son, your father's instruction and do not forsake your mother's teaching; indeed, they are a graceful wreath to your head and ornaments about your neck.

Notice that the teaching of both father and mother are praised. They are compared to a wreath, which symbolizes victory, as well as expensive ornaments, which can denote godly character. Our parents' training shapes us—for good or for bad. If they instill Christian virtues and moral values in us at an early age, we will be victorious in life as adults, and we will wear the priceless gold ornaments of honesty, purity, patience, integrity, faithfulness, and compassion. You can't buy ornaments like that; they are forged only through the fires of discipline.

Paul the apostle was very aware of the godly influence a Christian mother can make on her son. Paul wrote to his beloved disciple Timothy in 2 Timothy 1:5:

> For I am mindful of the sincere faith within you, which first dwelt in your grandmother Lois and your mother Eunice, and I am sure that it is in you as well.

Bible scholars don't know much about Timothy's upbringing, but they assume that his Gentile father was not a Christian. We don't know if Timothy grew up in a single-parent family or if his father provided any positive influence for him. What we do know is that Paul praised his mother's and grandmother's faith and credited them with leading Timothy to Christ. And we know that Paul cared for Timothy as if he were his own son (Phil. 2:22). Apparently Paul was able to fill any void Timothy suffered from the lack of a godly father.

I find it fascinating that Paul praises Lois and Eunice for their input into Timothy's life, and that his commendation was memorialized in the Bible. He specifically praises them for instilling biblical faith in the young man, who eventually became an apostolic leader in the early church. Many conservative Christians have assumed that because Paul once clamped down on a group of women in the church at Ephesus and forbid them to teach, Paul never allowed women access to the pulpit. Yet if we look at the women who served with Paul in gospel ministry, it is obvious that he empowered women and invited them to be a part of his team.

Let's consider the women who are specifically mentioned in the

New Testament. (This section is adapted from my book *25 Tough Questions About Women and the Church* [Charisma House, 2003].)

1. Priscilla

A skilled teacher who had been trained by Paul himself, Priscilla and her husband, Aquila, traveled throughout the Roman world strengthening newly established churches. The Bible often mentions her name before Aquila's, most likely because she had more of a visible teaching ministry. Some scholars believe that because she was Roman, she had more access to education than Jewish women in Palestine.

In Acts 18:18–21, we see Priscilla and Aquila instructing the man Apollos, who later became a powerful apostle in the early church. Apollos did not fully understand the message of the gospel, so Priscilla and her husband adjusted his theology and reshaped his message. She emerges as one of the true spiritual mothers of the early church period, and Paul was proud to call her a "fellow worker" in Romans 16:3.

2. Phoebe

Phoebe is referred to as a deacon in Romans 16:1–2. The passage says, "I commend to you our sister Phoebe, who is a servant [*diakonos*] of the church which is at Cenchrea" (v. 1). The word *diakonos* is always translated "minister" or "deacon" when applied to men, but the word is curiously translated in this verse as "servant" in the New American Standard Bible and other versions. This could be because Bible translators injected their own biases into the text. They simply assumed deacons could not be women.

In Romans 16:2, Paul refers to Phoebe as a *prostatis*, which can be translated "presiding officer." The term definitely carries with it a significant weight of authority, so we can conclude that Phoebe was not just teaching a women's Bible study class or setting up a vacation Bible school for kids. She was an apostolic envoy for Paul, and she had been sent to carry out his directives. Paul expected the church to listen to her. Bible scholar Catherine Kroeger notes that *prostatis* is often used in the writings of the early church fathers to denote a person who presided over communion.[6]

3. Nympha

Nympha is mentioned by Paul in Colossians 4:15. He asked the leaders of the Colossian church to "greet...Nympha and the church that is in her house." Traditionalists have argued that this woman was simply "hosting" the church meeting while men carried out all pastoral and teaching ministry, but then this begs the question: Why did Paul mention her rather than the male leaders who were presumably in charge? Was she just a hostess, making the tea and cookies for Paul and his team? Was Paul simply fond of Nympha because she knew how to cook his favorite meal? It is more probable that she had been designated to lead the church that met in her home.

However, if we suggest that Nympha was a pastor, we trigger a divisive debate, since some Christians believe the Bible totally limits this office to men. But does it? In Ephesians 4:11, where Paul explains that Jesus gave pastors, teachers, evangelists, apostles, and prophets to the church for its edification, he makes no rules about gender. The "no women pastors" rule—so common in many denominations today—is a religious tradition, not a biblical mandate.

4. Lydia

An influential, first-century businesswoman, Lydia became the first European convert to Christianity. Because she was wealthy and politically connected, it is most likely that she played a role in securing Paul's release from the Philippian magistrates. (In Acts 16:40 we learn that upon his release from jail, Paul returned to Lydia's house and demanded a trial.) Some scholars suggest that Lydia's story is included in the Book of Acts because she eventually pastored a church in her home and became a strategic member of Paul's apostolic team as he pushed the gospel westward, past Italy and all the way to Spain.

5. Junia

Junia was obviously a respected leader in the New Testament church. Up until the thirteenth century, no one questioned the name of this woman mentioned in Romans 16:7. Junia was a common name for a Roman woman at that time. However, Bible translators later began changing her name to a masculine form, "Junias" or "Junianus," because they could not accept the possibility that Paul would affirm a woman as an apostle. Actually, he says she is "outstanding among the apostles."

The original Greek manuscripts list her name correctly, and we don't need to adjust the spelling to fit our chauvinism. Paul singled this woman out because of her apostolic courage and for the fact that she suffered for her faith in prison alongside Paul. We don't have a record of her ministry accomplishments, but we can assume that she was involved in preaching and church planting.

Even early church father John Chrysostom (A.D. 347–407), who was by no means sympathetic to women, acknowledged that Junia held a powerful position in the New Testament church. He wrote in his commentary on Romans, "Indeed to be an apostle at all is a great thing; but to be even amongst those of note: Just consider what a great encomium that is. Oh, how great is the devotion of this woman, that she should be counted worthy of the appellation of Apostle."[7]

6. Euodia and Syntyche

Euodia and Syntyche were two women ministers mentioned by Paul in Philippians 4:2–3. He refers to them as "fellow workers" "who have shared my struggle" (v. 3). It is possible that they had been imprisoned with him in a crude Greek jailhouse, or perhaps they endured a difficult journey with Paul through Aegean waters. Whatever the case, they were definitely not just female members of the church at Philippi. They were leaders, and they were having a serious disagreement—so serious that Paul had to urge them to "live in harmony in the Lord" (v. 2).

We don't know why these women didn't get along. Perhaps their disagreement was over methodology or a minor point of doctrine, or perhaps they allowed jealousy or personal ambition to drive a wedge between them. We will never know what caused the tension between these two women, but we do know that Paul did not scold them because of their gender. He didn't say, "Tell those women that they don't have any business in the ministry. Women are too petty and emotional to be pastors." If Paul did not support women in such roles he would never have commended them as ministry colleagues.

We should also remember that in the old covenant, when God limited the Hebrew priesthood to an elite group of males who were descendants of Aaron, women emerged as powerful instruments in God's hand. Yet even in that dispensation He chose to use women. When God called Abram to be the father of the Jewish nation and changed his name to Abraham, He also called his wife and changed her name from Sarai to Sarah; she became a "mother of many nations." When He called Moses to lead the people of Israel through the wilderness, he also called his sister, Miriam, to a leadership position (Micah 6:4).

The prophet Deborah was single-handedly responsible for rallying the tribes of Israel to volunteer for battle against the Canaanites (Judg. 4), and her bravery spurred the Israelite army to an impressive, supernatural victory. Then a young Jewish woman named Jael put the exclamation point on the story by killing Sisera, the fugitive leader of the Canaanite army. When he came to Jael's tent looking for asylum, she put him to sleep and then nailed a tent peg into his skull with a hammer. The Bible makes it clear that Deborah's courage and Jael's cunning were strategic in securing Israel's military triumph. The women were given their proper credit even in a male-dominant culture.

Hannah was another influential spiritual mother during Old Testament times. Although she was barren, she asked God for a son so that he could grow up to be a prophet. She was concerned about the welfare of her nation, and she wanted a true prophet to confront the compromise and wickedness in Israel. When she went to the temple to pray, Eli, the priest in charge, ridiculed her for praying so passionately. He was clueless about what God was doing in Hannah, but God listened to her prayer. Her burden was rewarded when God gave her a promised son, Samuel, who ended up confronting Eli and the backslidden sons he had put in charge of God's house. And in the end, Hannah's prayer of victory became part of the Bible.

Another revered spiritual mother in the Old Testament is the prophet Huldah, who lived at the time of Jeremiah and offered counsel to King Josiah. At the time when she operated a small seminary in Jerusalem, most Israelites had turned away from God and turned to foreign idols. Few people remembered the Law of God anymore; in fact, copies of the Old Testament scrolls had been packed away in a storage closet in the temple. When some of King Josiah's deputies stumbled upon a copy of the Book of Deuteronomy and read about God's impending judgments, the king asked them to find someone in the city who understood spiritual things.

A priest named Hilkiah directed them to Huldah. She must have been the most spiritual person in Jerusalem at the time and the most aware of the true condition of the nation. We don't know that much about Huldah other than the fact that she was the keeper of the priestly wardrobe (2 Kings 22:14). She was probably not a wealthy woman. God's true prophets often tend to emerge from obscurity and then disappear just as fast.

But we do know that Huldah knew God. While the rest of the nation had been turning to idols, she had kept herself pure. While the rest of the nation had forgotten the Word of God, she was still studying it. She was no stranger to the forgotten book. Like any true mother, she was protective of Israel—but she was not afraid to rebuke the nation for its waywardness. When King Josiah's representative came to her seeking spiritual direction, she offered no flattery. She declared this prophetic message from God with authority:

Because they have forsaken Me and have burned incense to
other gods that they might provoke Me to anger with all the
works of their hands, therefore My wrath burns against this
place, and it shall not be quenched.

—2 KINGS 22:17

God blessed Huldah and mightily used her to speak to the king
of the nation and to the religious leaders of her day. He also pulled
women from total obscurity, such as Ruth and Esther, and rewarded
their faithfulness; these two women even have books of the Bible
named after them! And this was during the old covenant period,
before Christ ushered in a new day of freedom for women.

We as men must acknowledge that God not only uses women in
exceptional ways but also that we can personally benefit from their
ministry. Some men are like the hard-hearted Eli, who mocked
Hannah's righteous prayers and called her a drunkard. These men
think they are spiritually superior to women. Like the disrespectful
preachers who turned their backs on Billy Graham's daughter, they
would never listen to women preach because they don't think they
have anything worthwhile to say.

Other men are like the warrior Barak, who lived at the time of the
prophet Deborah. She called Barak to summon an army and go up
against the enemy, and he agreed on one condition: he said he would
not go unless Deborah went with him to the battlefield (Judg. 4:8).
Barak did not say this because he was a wimpy momma's boy. I am
sure he was a strong soldier endowed with plenty of military prowess.
But he recognized that Deborah was God's appointed prophet for
that time, and he knew Israel would not win the battle unless she was
there to command the victory in the spiritual realm.

Barak was not a coward. His request to have Deborah nearby was
not a sign of weakness. In fact, he is listed in the Book of Hebrews as
a true hero of faith (Heb. 11:32). But he realized that muscles, swords,

and chariots alone could not win this battle. His trust had to be in God alone. And Deborah helped him muster enough faith to believe.

I don't know about you, but I need women like that in my life. (That is why I am so blessed that my wife's name is Deborah.) I am not too proud to listen to a woman of God who has wise counsel from the Holy Spirit for me; in fact, I seek such counsel from my wife and from my spiritual mothers (as well as my spiritual fathers). Many Christian men make foolish mistakes because they don't listen to their wives when they sense danger around the corner. And many Christian men miss great blessings because they are too proud to listen to godly women who carry a message from the Lord. I pray you will not make that mistake.

Let's Talk About It

1. Do you believe the Bible limits the ways women can minister? If you were in a service with a woman preacher, would you turn your back to her like the men who protested Billy Graham's daughter? How would you respond?

2. Paul praised Timothy's grandmother and mother, Lois and Eunice, for instilling faith in the young man. Do you have any spiritual mothers in your life? How did they influence you positively?

3. Name some women in the New Testament who worked alongside Paul in the ministry. How did Paul treat these women?

4. Barak listened to the prophet Deborah and was blessed with a supernatural victory on the battlefield. Can you think of a time when you benefitted from the counsel of a godly woman?

WHAT ABOUT PAUL'S RESTRICTIONS ON WOMEN?

Many Christian leaders I know can quickly offer the names of several spiritual mothers who either led them to Christ or played a significant role in their spiritual formation. The influence of these women did not turn these men into sissies or lower their testosterone levels. You don't give up your masculinity when you listen to a godly woman. Most likely you will become a better man!

Hudson Taylor, a brave missionary pioneer who helped open up China to the gospel in the mid-1800s, said his mother and sister led him to the point of conversion. Billy Graham, one of the greatest evangelists of all time, and Bill Bright, the founder of the Campus Crusade for Christ movement, were both strongly influenced as teenagers by the stalwart Presbyterian Bible teacher Henrietta Mears, who led training conferences for youth in California in the 1940s.

When I first visited Nigeria in 2001, I interviewed Bishop David Oyedepo, whose Pentecostal church near Lagos, Winner's Chapel, was at that time the world's largest church building, with fifty thousand seats. When I asked him to share his testimony, he proudly shared that a white missionary woman from the Scripture Union organization led him to Jesus. (I am sure that woman did not live to see how her young convert would transform Nigeria.)

I hear this story frequently. In spite of the obstacles of male pride and stale religious tradition, God has been using His women, strategically placed, to win men to Christ, disciple them, teach them, counsel them, and inspire them.

But there is one problem. What do we do with Paul's instructions in 1 Timothy 2:12, in which he hands down a strict policy about women? If we read this passage by itself, without comparing it to other scriptures, it seems to contradict what the Bible says elsewhere. The passage reads this way in the King James Version:

But I suffer not a woman to teach, nor to usurp authority over the man, but to be in silence.

This is a curious passage indeed, and one that has puzzled many Bible scholars. It is confusing for several reasons:

- It seems to contradict how women have been used to speak for God in the Old Testament (as in the cases of Deborah and Huldah, for example).

- It does not seem to fit Paul's own practice, since he had women teachers (such as Priscilla) on his ministry team.

- In 1 Corinthians 11:5, Paul encourages women to pray and prophesy publicly in the local church meeting, and he invites the equal participation of all Christian believers in the exercising of spiritual gifts such as prophecy and the word of knowledge (1 Cor. 12:7–11).

So what is Paul saying in the 1 Timothy passage? If we take it at face value rather than compare it with other passages, we could conclude that women can never teach anyone, even small children. Some Christian denominations that limit women use this verse to restrict any form of "authoritative speech" that comes from women.

If this were the case, this would certainly rule out Huldah's prophecy to King Josiah. And it would also shut down Deborah's public ministry, since she went around to all the tribes of Israel and called them to battle. And what about the words of Deborah that are included in the canon of Scripture in Judges 4? Aren't her prophetic words "authoritative"? Traditionalists who believe Paul never allowed a woman to speak or hold positions of authority in a church are forced to play games with these passages of Scripture. This is why you will rarely hear one of these people preach a sermon about Deborah or Huldah.

But what do we do with Paul's words to Timothy? Here are two possible explanations why he had to "clamp down" on these women.

Possible scenario #1: The women in Ephesus needed more instruction.

Paul actually precedes his admonition in 1 Timothy 2:12 with is instruction in verse 11 (KJV):

> Let the woman learn in silence with all subjection.

That probably sounds sexist today, but let's remember that in the culture of first-century Asia Minor, women had been denied all schooling. Except for some wealthier Roman women, females in the Middle East were sequestered at home and kept away from books and learning. Illiteracy was the rule among women. The only thing men wanted them to learn was how to cook, tend to farm animals, and raise children.

Rabbis in this time period, in fact, believed it was blasphemous to teach a woman from the Torah. Jesus, of course, contradicted this view by inviting His women followers to sit at His feet and learn from Him. And here in 1 Timothy, Paul adopts Jesus's approach by encouraging the women to learn. Yet he calls them to learn in the proper way—not as know-it-alls but with a teachable spirit.

It is possible that the newly converted women in Ephesus were jumping the gun and trying to teach the gospel when they had not learned it first. We all know that would be disastrous. If such a free-for-all spirit had continued, Paul would have had to put his foot down and say, "Enough is enough. Women aren't allowed to teach until they know what they're talking about."

Notice that Paul also mentions the deception of Eve in the Garden of Eden. Perhaps he is reminding these misguided Ephesian women that they have a lot to learn from Eve. Because she acted independently of Adam when listening to the serpent, her failure triggered a crisis. Eve was not prepared to be a teacher, but she acted like one.

The question remains, Was Paul laying down a permanent rule for all time that forbids all women from teaching and exercising godly authority? Or was he issuing a correction that only applied to this situation? Since we know that Paul authorized other women like Priscilla to teach the Bible, we must conclude that his words were to correct the situation at hand. After all, if Paul called the women of Ephesus to learn "in all submissiveness" the Word of God, then surely he expected them to become mature disciples who would eventually have the ability to teach others after sufficient training.

Possible scenario #2: The church in Ephesus was disturbed by false teachers, and some of them were female.

Ephesus was a seat of paganism and was overrun by idolatry and heresies of every imaginable variety. It was a city full of cultism, Gnostic sects, and bizarre sexual practices. Archeology has proven that it was a headquarters for the worship of Artemis, a mystic religion involving moon worship and ritual prostitution. Timothy had quite a challenging assignment when he was sent to plant a church in this wicked city.

One theory of 1 Timothy 2:11–14 suggests that false teachers had infiltrated the infant church in Ephesus and were leading people astray with myths and false teachings. They were teaching such notions as (1) women are superior to men, (2) Eve was created before Adam and was a type of "mother goddess," (3) women don't need to get married or have children, and (4) Eve actually "liberated" the world from God's power when she listened to the serpent in the Garden of Eden. (Sounds a lot like the modern variety of militant feminism.) These false teachers were turning the Bible upside down and twisting the truth.

This would explain why Paul stepped in and put an end to this foolishness. He clamped down on the false doctrines and forbid these women from teaching their heresies. He also set the record straight about Eve by explaining that Adam was created first and that the woman fell into deception when she listened to the serpent. Paul said in 1 Timothy 2:13–14 (KJV):

> For Adam was first formed, then Eve. And Adam was not deceived, but the woman being deceived was in the transgression.

We also must note that 1 Timothy 2:12 does not say women cannot have authority (even though some Bible versions translate it this way). The King James Version says the women are not to "usurp" authority. The Greek word for "usurp" is *authentein*, and it is only used this once in the New Testament—leading us to believe it has a very narrow definition. It is a very violent word that means "to dominate" or even "to murder." It implies an attempt to overthrow established authority. It can even refer to ritual castration.[8]

Whatever was going on in Ephesus, we can be certain that it fit the category of blasphemy. The teachings of these women contradicted the Bible, twisted the order of creation, and redefined and overthrew traditional sex roles—an obvious goal of the worshipers of Artemis, who promoted sexual perversion. Certainly we should never allow such false doctrines to be proclaimed from our pulpits today.

However, we cannot use the passage in 1 Timothy 2:12 to suggest that trained, Spirit-empowered women cannot teach the Scriptures with authority. Nor can we say that women who have been graced with Spirit-endued gifts of leadership, pastoral anointing, or teaching ability must limit their teaching to women only. Men who receive instruction from such women will not be emasculated; on the contrary, they will grow stronger in Christ.

I believe it is time for godly male leaders in the church to become secure enough in their manhood to give these women a platform.

Let's Talk About It

1. The issue of women leaders seems very divisive. Why do you think it is that way?
2. Read 1 Timothy 2:11–15. How have you interpreted this verse in the past?
3. Some scholars believe the women in Ephesus had been denied education and were not ready to become teachers. Do you feel this is a possible interpretation?
4. Other scholars believe some female false teachers had infiltrated the Ephesian church. How would you handle that situation if you were in Paul's shoes?
5. How should you treat women who have been anointed by God and trained to be in the ministry?

Let's Pray About It

Father, thank You for the godly women You have put in my life. Forgive me if I have ever criticized a woman of God who was called by You, just because she was female. Forgive me for having a chauvinistic attitude toward my sisters in Christ. Give me the attitude of the apostle Paul, who commended the women on his team. Give me the heart of Jesus, who sent His women followers to be the first witnesses of His resurrection. Make me a champion for women! Amen.

10 𝕷𝕴𝕰𝕾

THE JOURNEY FROM WIMP TO WARRIOR

IKE SO MANY typical churchgoing guys, Ben admitted to me that he struggles in his relationship with God. He tries to maintain a consistent prayer life, but too often he sleeps through his alarm and ends up having morning devotions during his harried commute to work. He made Bible study a goal at one time, but he kept falling asleep while reading because he felt so tired after a long day at the office.

Then there was that nagging problem of lust. Ben once confessed to a friend at church that he often peeked at online pornography. What he didn't admit was that he regularly entertained sexual fantasies—and that his impure thoughts triggered continual guilt. As a result of his shame he often withholds feelings from his wife, which is causing an uneasy coldness in his marriage.

Sound familiar? If Ben's predicament isn't your own, I'm sure you know some guys who have similar problems. As I have spoken in various churches throughout the United States during recent years, I've met hundreds of guys like Ben—guys who want to please God but who feel they've sunk too deep in their own failures to reclaim their lost spirituality.

Many men live their Christian lives in the proverbial hamster's cage, running on a wheel and going nowhere. They're convinced that God must be ready to give up on them, if He hasn't already. Because they view God in this distorted way, they back away from His mercy rather than pursuing it.

As a result, a huge percentage of God's men are spiritually debilitated. They've disqualified themselves. The shame that hangs around their necks gets heavier by the day, so that they eventually become immobilized. And that's just where the devil wants them.

In recent years some strong voices have been calling out to Christian men, beckoning them to come out of this defeated position. The Promise Keepers organization emerged in the 1990s, challenging men to crawl out of the pit of failure by renewing their spiritual commitments and by acknowledging their need for moral accountability. A few years later, author John Eldredge challenged us to reclaim our latent masculinity by learning how to be "wild at heart," the title of his now popular book.

Gordon Dalbey, author of *Healing the Masculine Soul,* did groundbreaking work on the issue of why we men struggle so much to find significance and approval. And author Steve Arterburn challenged Christian men to wrestle their sexual addictions by facing what he aptly called *Every Man's Battle.*

I agree with Promise Keepers, Eldredge, Dalbey, and Arterburn that Christian men must climb out of this pit and get ruthless with our sin. But I also know that many men who stood at the altars at Promise Keepers rallies and vowed to walk in faithfulness to God are now struggling again. A guy can try his best to become "wild at heart," but this doesn't guarantee that his recharged masculinity will translate into any measurable spiritual victory.

Frankly, I think it's odd that we as Christian men go hunting in Colorado, fly fishing in Vermont, or horseback riding in North Dakota in order to reclaim our lost sense of masculine adventure. As much as I support efforts to get men free from lust, I don't think the battle can be won just by talking about the problem or by counting how many times you masturbated in the last week.

We're missing something: Jesus already commissioned us to the greatest adventure and the greatest battle of all time. He called us to reach all nations with the gospel. He called us to share Christ with others. He called us to claim spiritual territory for Him. That is truly "every man's battle!" It is by enlisting in that battle—and by determining that we will be used by God in the lives of others—that we break this cycle of spiritual defeat.

The challenge of ministering to a lost world should be enough to make us wild at heart. After you have led someone to the Lord, helped a guy overcome a life-controlling problem, or fed hungry people in a developing country, you simply don't have time to fool with your puny little problems.

THE CALL TO WAR

I was eighteen years old when I gave my life to Christ and asked Jesus to fill me with the Holy Spirit. A few days later I experienced what I know understand was a supernatural vision. At the time, I thought I was just seeing some vivid Technicolor thoughts.

In this vision I was riding on a horse, and Jesus was riding on His steed in front of me. Both of us were dressed in primitive armor, complete with swords, shields, and bronze helmets. We were criss-crossing what looked like an ancient battlefield, and I had the sense that I was serving Jesus as an apprentice warrior.

When we arrived at our camp, Jesus unfolded a leather map and began to point at various places as He explained tomorrow's battle strategy. I remember thinking at the time, "This is so awesome! I get to actually be with Jesus in the battle." Being near to Him was the most thrilling part of the whole vision.

It would be several years before I would read any books about spiritual warfare or come to understand that Christians have been given authority in the cosmic conflict with hell's forces. Yet this vision marked my life immediately. I knew from that moment on that I had been called by God to engage in this war and that Jesus would lead me every step of the way.

My first spiritual battles were fought in college, when I was part of a campus ministry that was aggressively winning students to the Lord. I learned in those days that there is nothing more exciting than seeing someone give his or her heart to Christ. Later, after I began a career in journalism, I tried to stay active in lay ministry, whether it was leading a home group in my church, discipling younger guys, or simply sharing my faith with people who didn't know God.

In more recent years, the Lord challenged me to step outside of my comfort zone and start speaking in churches and conferences. At first I tried to employ every imaginable excuse for avoiding the call of God, such as, "Lord, I'm not the right guy for this assignment. You know I can't preach well enough. You know I shouldn't travel away from my family. Yadda, yadda, yadda."

In the end, I surrendered. First I started doing weekend trips in the United States. Then doors opened overseas. From 2001 to 2009 I had preached in twenty-four countries. Today the thrill of seeing people's lives changed is so much of a rush that it keeps me up at night.

My travels have taken me to every continent except Antarctica. God has opened doors for me to speak to underground Chinese evangelists, abused Bolivian women, crowds in Ukraine, and a group of eight thousand Nigerian pastors. And the more I step out into the unknown and allow God to use me, the more passionate I become about the Great Commission. I'm dreaming now about the doors He will open to me in the Middle East.

I can't seem to get enough of the adventure—even though international travel is tiresome and expensive. While I used to say, "Not me, Lord," now I say, "Here I am, Lord. Send me!"

We must adopt this kind of mind-set in order to walk in personal victory. Some people might be tempted to think that I can preach all over the world because I have it all together. Wrong! I could give you a long list of fears, temptations, and weaknesses I struggle with. In fact, I am plagued with insecurities. But I have learned to see myself as a warrior rather than as the wimp I used to be. When I see myself in light of what the Bible says about me, I am catapulted into a new realm of victory over sin.

That doesn't mean I never stumble. Whenever I feel overwhelmed by temptation, I confess my failures to a trusted friend. Godly accountability is a powerful weapon in the battle for personal holiness.

But I have learned that all the accountability in the world will not work for you if you have not adopted a ministry mind-set. You can't win this battle just sitting on the sidelines (or in a church pew). It's only when you get in the trenches with other warriors that you will find a real breakthrough.

In recent years I have gleaned deep inspiration from some men in the Bible who were godly warriors. These guys get me excited, because I know their lives were designed by God to be models for us.

1. Joshua, a timid man who became valiant

Joshua was most likely a timid guy, because God often challenged him to be "strong and courageous" (Josh. 1:6–7, 9). God said this three times when He called Joshua to lead the army of Israel. Yet after Joshua had an encounter with "the captain of the host of the LORD" (Josh. 5:13–15) he led God's people through endless battles. In fact, he never stopped fighting, even in his old age.

Joshua reminds me that I cannot fight in my own strength, but if I listen to the Lord and stay close to His heart, I will be able to evict devils from their hideouts and claim territory for God's kingdom. If you don't have a warrior mentality, perhaps it is because you have not encountered Jesus as your mighty Captain.

2. Gideon, an insecure man who became a commander

Gideon had a serious inferiority complex. When the angel of the Lord came to him and said, "Hail, O valiant warrior!" (Judg. 6:12), his response was basically, "Who, me?" Gideon was in a defeated position at the time. He was threshing his grain in a hole in the ground so the enemies couldn't attack him. He was in a total defensive posture and felt overwhelmed. He was the last guy any of us would have picked for a winning team.

But after Gideon encountered the fire of God at the altar of sacrifice, he was transformed into another man. He stormed into His father's house, tore down the idolatrous images of Baal and Asherah, and then stood up to his relatives who threatened to kill him. Then he led a scraggly band of three hundred men to overthrow the enemies of Israel. God can turn wimps into warriors!

3. David, the passionate giant-killer

David's life is full of lessons for us men. His valor in the face of Goliath reminds us that we too are called to attack demonic giants—even when other Christians seem intimidated by the prospect of conflict. David's life gives me courage in the face of any false religion or spiritual force that keeps people from knowing the truth of the gospel.

David's failures also provide some important insights. The reason he fell into adultery with Bathsheba was because he had left the battlefield and was sitting on his roof while all the other soldiers were fighting. If he had been where he was supposed to be instead of abdicating his position, he wouldn't have seen Bathsheba taking her clothes off. And he would have avoided the biggest ethical and moral blunder of his life.

Do you believe God can make you a giant-killer? Your future is not determined by your present condition. You may feel timid like Joshua, or you may wrestle with an inferiority complex like Gideon. Or perhaps you know you are called by God, yet you are out of position like David. God can make you a warrior even if you feel like a wimp today. You must simply allow Him to take you through His process. Then you must step out of your comfort zone and into the realm of spiritual adventure He has for you.

If you truly want to become a spiritual warrior, you must realize that you cannot do this in your own strength. Jesus never intended His followers to do the work of ministry on their own. He provided to us a means of supernatural empowerment. In the account of Gideon, we read that he saw God's fire fall from heaven after he gave an offering to the angel of the Lord (Judg. 6:21).

Many people in the Bible had similar encounters with God's fire. Moses heard God speaking to him from a burning bush. Abraham saw burning fire pots pass through the sacrifice he made. When Isaiah was called to be a prophet, an angel touched his lips with a burning coal from God's altar. After Jeremiah was called, he felt a spiritual fire in his bones. When Ezekiel saw a vision of heaven, he saw torches and lightning flashing from a fire.

In Scripture, fire is often a symbol of the Holy Spirit. When Jesus was about to ascend to heaven, He told His followers to wait in Jerusalem for the power of the Holy Spirit. Several weeks later, on the Day of Pentecost, that fire fell on the 120 disciples who had been praying together in an upper room. The Bible says they were all filled with the Holy Spirit. This experience changed them forever and ignited a supernatural anointing that gave the early church the ability to preach with boldness and to perform miracles.

If you want to embrace all that God has for you and become His warrior, you need this experience. You cannot be an effective warrior simply by memorizing Scripture, attending church, and reading your Bible—even though those things are essential. You must have a personal encounter with the fire of God. You must lay your life on His altar in total surrender and ask Him to fill you totally.

My friend, you can exchange your weakness for His strength. Let Him clothe you with His ability. He will make you the man of God you could never become on your own!

Let's Talk About it

1. How would you describe your spiritual condition today: (1) wimp, (2) warrior, or (3) somewhere in between? Why?

2. Are there any areas in your personal life or issues from your past that you feel have disqualified you from being used by God in a significant way? Talk about these.

3. If fear and doubt were not obstacles in your way, how could you step out into greater areas of ministry to others?

4. Have you been baptized with the Holy Spirit? If not, are you willing to pray this prayer and ask God to fill you with His supernatural power? In the following appendix you can find clear guidelines to help you take this important step in your spiritual journey.

Let's Pray About It

Father, I know You have called me to a spiritual battle. Please make me a true warrior. Forgive me for allowing fears, doubts, lust, pride, or shame to keep me from fulfilling my ministry to others. Enable me, by Your amazing grace, to rise above my weaknesses so that I can share the love of Jesus with others. Fill me with Your strength so that my life can be a true adventure. Amen.

10 LIES

EVERY MAN'S SECRET TO SPIRITUAL POWER

HAVE YOU EVER wanted to be truly "wild" for God? That has always been my desire. I don't want to live a status quo life. And I have learned that the secret to becoming a spiritual powerhouse is to embrace the baptism of the Holy Spirit.

Hundreds of years before the Holy Spirit was poured out on the early church on the Day of Pentecost, the Old Testament prophet Ezekiel, newly anointed as a priest, got a free preview of how God would send the Holy Spirit to empower His people. The preview came in the form of a Technicolor vision that included a stormy wind, a cloud that glowed with fire, flashes of lightning, and strange, four-faced cherubim that were empowered by God's divine energy.

Ezekiel wrote of these heavenly creatures, "In the midst of the living beings there was something that looked like burning coals of fire, like torches darting back and forth among the living beings. The fire was bright, and lightning was flashing from the fire. And the living beings ran to and fro like bolts of lightning" (Ezek. 1:13–14).

Ezekiel also got a close-up view of these angelic creatures. They each had four faces and four wings. Their feet, which looked like calves' hooves, seemed to glow like bronze (v. 7). And the fantastical creatures had the faces of a bull, a lion, an eagle, and a man. Sounds like something you might see in a sci-fi movie or read about in a J. R. R. Tolkien novel, but this is in the Bible. It is a pre-Pentecost look at Pentecost.

I used to dismiss Ezekiel's amazing vision as nothing more than a description of strange-looking angels in heaven, but now I realize more is implied in the prophet's vision. The four-faced creatures are described in detail to remind us that anyone who is anointed by the Holy Spirit will be transformed into something wild! These animals represent qualities of God's nature that He shares with us.

The "living creatures" Ezekiel saw had the face of man. This symbolizes human nature. All of us are frail vessels of clay, and we will always deal with flaws, temptations, and weaknesses. But the creatures also had the faces of three wild animals. This signifies to us that when we are filled with God's Holy Spirit, He shares with us His supernatural attributes. Our very nature is infused with a raw, holy zeal.

The bull speaks of spiritual strength. It is what the psalmist had in mind when he wrote, "You have exalted my horn like that of the wild ox; I have been anointed with fresh oil" (Ps. 92:10). When the oil of the Spirit touches us, we receive rare, unexplainable power to accomplish what we could not do before. We are able to advance in the Spirit and take territory for the Lord.

The lion speaks of evangelistic courage. As Proverbs 28:1 says, "The wicked flee when no one is pursuing, but the righteous are as bold as a lion." This animal fears nothing and no one. His roar is the loudest sound in the jungle. Truly Spirit-empowered Christians cannot stop talking about Jesus.

The eagle speaks of missionary speed as well as keen prophetic insight. The prophet Isaiah understood this when he said that "those who wait for the LORD will gain new strength; they will mount up with wings like eagles, they will run and not get tired, they will walk and not become weary" (Isa. 40:31).

What God was showing Ezekiel was the miracle of Pentecost, when God would clothe His people with power from on high. Not only would the early disciples hear the sound of a rushing wind and see flames of fire descend on every believer's head. Those believers would be infused with untamable qualities—supernatural strength, fierce courage, uncanny boldness, and an unusual ability to see into the invisible realm of God's mysteries.

When I say that the Holy Spirit is wild, I am not suggesting that He brings disorder or chaos. God is not the author of confusion or silliness. But too often the American church has tried to put the third person of the Trinity in a box. We want to confine Him, muzzle Him, constrain Him, or shoot Him with a tranquilizer gun so we can maintain control.

God wants to transform you. He wants to make you lionhearted. He wants to fill you with so much of His power that you break out of your normal routine and become an adventurer. This will happen when you are baptized in the Holy Spirit.

TAKE A BOLD STEP

When we meet Christ and put our trust in Him, we are "born again" (John 3:3) and we receive the Holy Spirit in our hearts. This is the most important decision we will ever make. This happened to the disciples of Jesus in John 20:22, which says, "[Jesus] breathed on them and said to them, 'Receive the Holy Spirit.'"

But before Jesus ascended to heaven, He told His disciples to wait in Jerusalem until the promise of the Father had come (Luke 24:49). He told them that if they would wait there, they would be "clothed with power from on high." In Acts 1:8 Jesus told His followers that they would receive "power" to be His witnesses.

So the disciples waited in Jerusalem for many days, praying near the temple. On the Day of Pentecost, which was fifty days after Jesus had died on the cross, something amazing happened. The Holy Spirit was poured out on the early church. This is described in Acts 2:1–4. The Bible says that when the Spirit came, the disciples were filled (another word is *baptized*) with the Spirit.

This shows us that there are two separate experiences we can have with God. One is salvation, in which we receive God's amazing forgiveness and a new nature. The Holy Spirit comes to live inside us, and He becomes our teacher, our comforter, and our helper.

The second experience is the baptism of the Holy Spirit, in which the Holy Spirit, who is already in us, overflows. To be "baptized in the Spirit" means "completely immersed in the Spirit." Jesus never wanted us to rely on our own ability to do the work of ministry. He wants to do it through us. So He fills us with the Holy Spirit in order to empower us with His ability.

When we have this experience, the Holy Spirit's power fills us so full that He spills out. Also, when we are baptized in the Spirit, unusual "gifts of the Holy Spirit"—which are listed in 1 Corinthians 12:8–10—begin to be manifested in our lives. We begin to experience His supernatural power. These gifts include prophecy, discernment, miracles, healing, and speaking in unknown tongues.

When people were baptized in the Holy Spirit in the New Testament church, the Bible says they all spoke in tongues (Acts 2:1–4; 4:31; 10:44–48; 19:1–7). A lot of people get hung up on speaking in tongues because it seems like a weird thing. It's actually not strange at all. It is a very special form of prayer that any Christian can experience.

When we pray in our heavenly prayer language, we are praising God and also strengthening ourselves spiritually. Speaking in tongues helps us become mighty in the Spirit. The apostle Paul, truly a giant in the New Testament church, told the Corinthian believers, "I thank God, I speak in tongues more than you all" (1 Cor. 14:18).

Being baptized in the Holy Spirit is not something you have to qualify for. Any Christian can ask, and Jesus is ready to do it. You can pray by yourself, or you can ask someone else to pray for you.

Here are the simple steps you can take to be filled with the Holy Spirit:

1. **Prepare your heart.** The Holy Spirit is holy. He is compared to a fire (Matt. 3:11), which means He purifies sin and burns up that which is not Christlike in our lives. Make sure you have confessed all known sin and made your heart ready for His infilling.

2. **Ask Jesus to baptize you in the Spirit.** You do not need to jump through hoops to get God's attention. He is eager to answer your request. Jesus is the one who baptizes us in the Spirit, so ask Him—and expect Him to answer.

3. **Receive the infilling.** Begin to thank Him for this miracle. The Holy Spirit's power is filling your life. If you feel your mind is clouded with doubts, just praise the Lord. Focus your mind on Him and not on yourself.

4. **Release your prayer language.** The moment you are filled with the Spirit, you will receive the ability to speak in your heavenly prayer language. You may feel the words bubbling up inside of you. You may begin to hear the words in your mind. Open your mouth and began to speak, trusting the Lord to give you this new, supernatural language.

5. **Step out in boldness.** After you have been baptized in the Holy Spirit, one of the first things you will notice is a new boldness. The Holy Spirit does not like to hide. He wants you to speak about Jesus to those around you—and He will give you surprising courage.

NOTES

LIE #1
GOD MADE MEN SUPERIOR TO WOMEN.

1. Aristotle, *Politics*, trans. Benjamin Jowett, The Internet Classics Archive, http://classics.mit.edu/Aristotle/politics.1.one.html (accessed September 22, 2010).

2. "Where Do You Suppose Dr. Shedd Got His Opinion of Women?" FreeThinkers of Colorado Springs, http://www.freethinkerscs.com/articles/wheredoyousuppose.htm (accessed June 15, 2010).

3. John Wijngaards, "Greek Philosophy on the Inferiority of Women," Women Can Be Priests website, http://www.womenpriests.org/traditio/infe_gre.asp (accessed September 22, 2010).

4. The Quran, M. H. Shakir Translation, http://www.muslimaccess.com/quraan/translations/shakir/004.htm (accessed June 15, 2010).

5. Reform Gilbert Haggadah, "Morning Prayer," *The Standard Prayer Book; Authorized English Translation*, trans. Simeon Singer (New York: Bloch Publishing Company, 1915), http://www.archive.org/stream/standardprayerbo-00hagg/
standardprayerbo00hagg_djvu.txt (accessed June 18, 2010).

6. Samuel Butler, Miscellaneous Thoughts, http://www.giga-usa.com/quotes/authors/samuel_butler_1_a008.htm (accessed June 15, 2010).

7. Freidoune Sahebjam, *The Stoning of Soraya M* (n.p.: Arcade Publishing, 1995).

8. *The Stoning of Soraya M.*, dir. Cyrus Nowrasteh (n.p.: Lions Gate Films Home Entertainment, 2010), DVD.

9. L. Heise, M. Ellsberg, and M. Gottemoeller, "Ending Violence Against Women," *Population Reports*, series L, no. 11 (December 1999).

10. Tracy Wilkinson, "United Nations Commission Reports on Violence Against Women in Latin America," *Los Angeles Times*, November 25, 2009.

11. United States Department of State, "Trafficking in Persons Report: June 2005" (Washington DC: United States Department of State, 2005).

12. International Organization for Migration (IOM) Kosovo, Counter Trafficking Unit, "Return and Reintegration Project, Situation Report" (Pristina: IOM, 2001).

13. International Organization for Migration, "New IOM Figures on the Global Scale of Trafficking," *Trafficking in Migrants Quarterly Bulletin* (Geneva: IOM, 2001).

14. United Nations Population Fund, "India: Restoring the Sex-Ration Balance," www.unfpa.org/culture/case_studies/india_study.htm (accessed October 1, 2010).

15. C. Watts and C. Zimmerman, "Violence Against Women: Global Scope and Magnitude," *The Lancet* 359 (April 6, 2002). The barbaric practice of genital mutilation is sometimes called female circumcision, but it cannot be fairly compared to male circumcision. The cutting off of the male foreskin does not decrease sexual pleasure, nor does it cause health risks. In fact, male circumcision—which was instituted by God with the patriarch Abraham—actually offers health benefits.

16. Ibid.

17. The United Nations Population Fund (UNFPA) estimates that the annual worldwide total of honor-killing victims may be as high as five thousand. The number is really not obtainable because these kinds of murders are carried out secretly and are rarely reported.

18. Manuel Bermúdez, "Guatemala: Violence Against Women Unchecked and Unpunished," Inter Press Service, November 25, 2005, www.ipsnews.net.

19. Prega Govender, "Child Rape: A Taboo Within the AIDS Taboo; More and More Girls Are Being Raped by Men Who Believe This Will 'Cleanse' Them of the Disease, but People Don't Want to Confront the Issue," *Sunday Times,* South Africa, April 4, 1999, http://www.aegis.com/news/suntimes/1999/ST990401.html (accessed June 15, 2010).

20. Ibid.

LIE #2
A MAN CANNOT BE CLOSE TO HIS FATHER.

1. "Eminem Quotes," ThinkExist.com http://thinkexist.com/quotes/like/my_father-i_never_knew_him-never_even_seen_a/342583/ (accessed June 15, 2010).

2. "Michael Jackson: In His Own Words," *The Sunday Times*, June 26, 2009, accessed June 15, 2010, http://entertainment.timesonline.co.uk/tol/arts_and_entertainment/music/article6581704.ece.

3. Dave Simmons, *Dad, the Family Counselor* (n.p.: Victor Books, 1991), as quoted in http://www.diyfather.com/content/Men_who_hate_their_fathers (accessed September 22, 2010).

4. *The Cable Guy*, dir. Ben Stiller (1996; n.p.: Columbia TriStar Home Video, n.d.), DVD.

5. "Corey Taylor; Metal Hammer," SlipKnot-Metal.com, http://www .slipknot-metal.com/main.php?sk=quotes (accessed June 15, 2010). Be advised that this website contains explicit language.

6. Jack Frost, *Experiencing the Father's Embrace* (Lake Mary, FL: Charisma House, 2002).

7. D. James Kennedy, "Restoring the Soul of the Nation," *Issues Tearing Our Nation's Fabric* (Fort Lauderdale, FL: Center for Reclaiming America, 1997), http://www.leaderu.com/issues/fabric/chap03.html (accessed June 22, 2010).

8. Ibid.

9. Janice Shaw Crouse, "Family Breakdown and the Nation's Pocketbook," AmericanThinker.com, February 20, 2010, http://www.americanthinker .com/2010/02/family_breakdown_and_the_natio.html (accessed June 22, 2010).

10. *Dead Poets Society*, dir. Peter Weir (1989; n.p.: Buena Vista Home Entertainment, 1998), DVD.

11. *The Blind Side*, dir. John Lee Hancock (2009; n.p.: Warner Home Video, 2010), DVD.

LIE #3
A REAL MAN IS DEFINED BY MATERIAL SUCCESS.

1. *Scarface*, dir. Brian De Palma (1983; n.p.: Universal Home Entertainment, 1998), DVD.

2. "Donald Trump Quotes," ThinkExist.com, http://thinkexist.com/ quotation/i_wasn-t_satisfied_just_to_earn_a_good_living-i/327079.html (accessed June 15, 2010).

3. *Wall Street*, dir. Oliver Stone (1987; n.p.: Twentieth Century Fox Home Entertainment, 2000), DVD.

4. "James Cameron Accepting the Oscar for Directing Titanic—70th Annual Academy Awards," YouTube, video posted March 14, 2008, http:// www.youtube.com/watch?v=xJp7Wd6Af2A (accessed June 15, 2010).

5. "Success Quotes," AYearFromNow.com, http://www.ayearfromnow.com/ success-quotes.html (access June 15, 2010).

6. Luisa Kroll and Matthew Miller, eds., "The World's Billionaires," *Forbes* magazine, March 10, 2010, accessed June 21, 2010, http://www.forbes. com/2010/03/10/worlds-richest-people-slim-gates-buffett-billionaires-2010_ land.html.

7. Kenneth Barker, ed., *NASB Zondervan Study Bible* (Grand Rapids, MI: Zondervan Publishing House, 1999), 1370.

LIE #4
A MAN IS THE ULTIMATE "BOSS" OF HIS FAMILY.

1. John Knox, *The First Blast of the Trumpet Against the Monstrous Regiment of Women* (extract) (Geneva, 1558), http://picard.montclair.edu/~landwebj/wpp/knox_blast.htm (accessed June 15, 2010).

2. "Where Do You Suppose Dr. Shedd Got His Opinion of Women?" Freethinkers of Colorado Springs, http://www.freethinkerscs.com/articles/wheredoyousuppose.htm (accessed June 15, 2010).

3. "Glover Cleveland Quotes," ThinkExist.com, http://thinkexist.com/quotation/sensible_and_responsible_women_do_not_want_to/206690.html (accessed June 16, 2010).

4. "Quote #464," Witty Quotes Haven: All Witty Sayings, http://www.witty-quotes.com/all_24.html (accessed June 16, 2010).

5. "Famous Quotes About Women and Marriage," 3roms.com, http://www.3roms.com/forums/showthread.php?p=35387 (accessed June 16, 2010).

6. "Groucho Marx Quotes," ThinkExist.com, http://de.thinkexist.com/quotes/groucho_marx/ (accessed June 16, 2010).

7. "Housework," Quoteland.com, http://www.quoteland.com/rate.asp?QUOTE_ID=6629 (accessed June 16, 2010).

8. *The Stepford Wives*, directed by Brian Forbes (1975; Embassy Home Entertainment, n.d.), VHS.

LIE #5
SEX IS PRIMARILY FOR THE MAN'S ENJOYMENT, NOT THE WOMAN'S.

1. "Hugh Hefner Quotes," ThinkExist.com, http://thinkexist.com/quotation/i-always-say-now-that-i-m-in-my-blonde-years/551217.html (accessed June 16, 2010).

2. Jacqueline Kennedy Onassis quote, Famous Quotes About Adultery, http://www.famous-quotes.com/topic.php?tid=20 (accessed September 22, 2010).

3. "Lenore Coffe Quotes," WorldofQuotes.com, http://www.worldofquotes.com/author/Lenore-Coffee/1/index.html (accessed June 16, 2010).

4. "Kin Hubbard Quotes," BrainyQuote.com, http://www.brainyquote.com/quotes/quotes/k/kinhubbard106733.html (accessed June 16, 2010).

5. *Slumdog Millionaire*, dir. Danny Boyle and Loveleen Tandan (2008; n.p.: Twentieth Century Fox Home Entertainment, 2009), DVD.

6. William Barclay, *The Letter to the Corinthians* (Louisville, KY: Westminster John Knox Press, 1954), 2–3.

7. David Padfield, "Corinth, Greece in the New Testament," Padfield .com, http://www.padfield.com/2005/corinth.html (accessed June 22, 2010). Aphrodite is portrayed in statues as a beautiful, naked woman. She was the patron of prostitutes, and Greeks believed she was born when a Titan named Cronus cut off the god Uranus's genitals with a sickle and threw them into the sea. Many scholars believe Aphrodite was the Greek version of the Canaanite goddess Ashtoreth—a female counterpart to Baal that the back-slidden children of Israel worshiped.

LIE #6
IT'S OK FOR A MAN TO HIT OR ABUSE A WOMAN.

1. Julia Savacool, "Our Most Important Mission Ever: Stop Violence Against Women Now," MarieClaire.com, http://www.marieclaire.com/world -reports/news/latest/domestic-violence-stop (accessed June 16, 2010).

2. Ibid.

3. "Quotes From the Movie *Gone With the Wind*," FinestQuotes.com, http://www.finestquotes.com/movie_quotes/movie/Gone%20with%20the%20 Wind/page/0.htm (accessed June 16, 2010).

4. The Associated Press, "Marlon Brando Movie Quotes," USAToday.com, July 2, 2004, http://www.usatoday.com/life/movies/news/2004-07-02-brando -movie-quotes_x.htm (accessed June 16, 2010).

5. Rosie Swash, "Grammys 2009: Rihanna Cancels Appearance After Boyfriend Chris Brown Arrested," Guardian.co.uk, February 9, 2009, http://www.guardian.co.uk/music/2009/feb/09/grammy-awards-rihanna-chris -brown (accessed June 21, 2010).

6. George Rush and Nancy Dillon, "TMZ Posts Rihanna Photo Showing Star's Bruised Face After Alleged Chris Brown Beating," NYDailyNews.com, February 20, 2009, http://www.nydailynews.com/gossip/2009/02/19/2009 -02-19_tmz_posts_rihanna_photo_showing_stars_br.html (accessed June 21, 2010).

7. "Oprah 'Sends Love' to Chris Brown and Rihanna, Dedicates Show to Abuse," FoxNews.com, March 12, 2009, http://www.foxnews.com/ entertainment/2009/03/12/oprah-sends-love-chris-brown-rihanna-dedicates -abuse/ (accessed June 21, 2010).

8. Reader reactions, Rush and Dillon, "TMZ Posts Rihanna Photo Showing Star's Bruised Face After Alleged Chris Brown Beating."

9. Ibid.

10. Heise, Ellsberg, and Gottemoeller, "Ending Violence Against Women."

11. J. A. Gazmararian, R. Petersen, A. M. Spitz, M. M. Goodwin, L. E. Saltzman, and J. S. Marks, "Violence and Reproductive Health; Current Knowledge and Future Research Directions," *Maternal and Child Health Journal* 4, no. 2 (2002): 79–84; "Intimate Partner Violence, 1993–2001," Bureau of Justice Statistics Crime Data Brief (2003).

12. "Violence Against Women, A Majority Staff Report," Committee on the Judiciary United States Senate, 102nd Congress (n.p.: n.p., 1992), 3.

13. V. Frye, "Examining Homicide's Contribution to Pregnancy-Associated Deaths," *Journal of the American Medical Association* 285, no. 11 (2001).

14. J. G. Silverman, A. Raj, L. A. Mucci, and J. E. Hathaway, "Dating Violence Against Adolescent Girls and Associated Substance Abuse, Unhealthy Weight Control, Sexual Control, Sexual Risk Behavior, Pregnancy, and Suicidality," *Journal of the American Medical Association* 286, no. 5 (2001).

15. Patricia Tjaden and Nancy Thoennes, "Prevelence, Incidence, and Consequences of Violence Against Women: Findings from the National Violence Against Women Survey," National Institute of Justice: Center for Disease Control and Prevention, November 1998, http://www.ncjrs.gov/pdffiles/172837.pdf (accessed June 22, 2010).

16. E. Krug, et al., eds., "Women Are at Greatest Risk of Violence From Men They Know," *World Report on Violence and Health* (Geneva: WHO, 2002); as quoted in "Violence Against Women Fact Sheet," UNFPA.org, http://www.unfpa.org/swp/2005/presskit/factsheets/facts_vaw.htm#ftn6 (accessed June 22, 2010). In Australia, Canada, Israel, South Africa, and the United States, 40–70 percent of female murder victims were killed by their partners.

17. Chris Kubrin and Ronald Weitzer, "Misogyny in Rap Music: Objectification, Exploitation, and Violence against Women," paper presented at the annual meeting of the American Society of Criminology, Atlanta Marriott Marquis, Atlanta, Georgia, November 14, 2007, http://www.allacademic.com/meta/p200347_index.html (accessed June 22, 2010).

LIE #7
REAL MEN DON'T NEED CLOSE MALE FRIENDSHIPS.

1. Henry Wadsworth Longfellow, "The Theologian's Tale; Elizabeth," *Tales of a Wayside Inn*, IV (1863), http://www.hwlongfellow.org/poems_poem.php?pid=2074 (accessed November 18, 2010).

2. "Thomas Wolfe Quotes," ThinkExist.com, http://en.thinkexist.com/quotation/the_whole_conviction_of_my_life_now_rests_upon/163917.html (accessed June 17, 2010).

3. "Vincent van Gogh Quotes," ThinkExist.com, http://thinkexist.com/quotation/one_may_have_a_blazing_hearth_in_one-s_soul_and/144719.html (accessed June 17, 2010).

4. Bill Hybels, *Honest to God?* (Grand Rapids, MI: Zondervan, 1992).

5. "Wayne McLaren, 51, Rodeo Rider and Model," Obituaries, *New York Times*, July 25, 1992, accessed September 22, 2010, http://www.nytimes.com/1992/07/25/obituaries/wayne-mclaren-51-rodeo-rider-and-model.html; "Marlboro Manslaughter," Snopes.com, August 6, 2007, http://www.snopes.com/radiotv/tv/marlboro.asp (accessed September 22, 2010).

6. "The Marlboro Man," *Ad Age*, 2005, http://adage.com/century/icon01.html.

7. "Marlboro Man," Wikipedia, http://en.wikipedia.org/wiki/Marlboro_Man (accessed October 1, 2010). Three men who appeared in Marlboro advertisements, Wayne McLaren, David McLean, and Dick Hammer, all died of lung cancer, thus earning Marlboro cigarettes, specifically Marlboro Reds, the nickname "cowboy killers." McLaren testified in favor of anti-smoking legislation at the age of fifty-one, a year before he died.

8. David W. Smith, *The Friendless American Male* (n.p.: Regal Books, 1983), 23.

9. *Red Dawn*, dir. John Milius (1984; n.p.: MGM/UA Home Entertainment, 1998), DVD.

LIE #8
A MAN SHOULD NEVER ADMIT HIS WEAKNESSES.

1. "Tiger Woods: I Have Let My Family Down and I Regret Those Transgressions," TheInsider.com, December 2, 2009, http://www.theinsider.com/news/3097223_Tiger_Woods_I_Have_Let_My_Family_Down_and_I_Regret_Those_Transgressions (accessed June 17, 2010).

2. "At the White House News Conference on Education," WashingtonPost.com, January 26, 1998, http://www.washingtonpost.com/wp-srv/politics/special/clinton/stories/whatclintonsaid.htm (accessed June 17, 2010).

3. "Nationally Televised Speech," WashingtonPost.com, August 17, 1998, http://www.washingtonpost.com/wp-srv/politics/special/clinton/stories/whatclintonsaid.htm (June 17, 2010).

4. "Reverend Jimmy Swaggart: Apology Sermon," Family Worship Center, Baton Rouge, Louisiana, February 21, 1988, as quoted at *American Rhetoric* Online Speech Bank, http://www.americanrhetoric.com/speeches/jswaggartapologysermon.html (accessed June 17, 2010).

5. Mark Twain, *Following the Equator* (n.p.: n.d.).

6. "Edgar Watson Howe Quotes," http://thinkexist.com/quotation/the_man_who_can_keep_a_secret_may_be_wise-but_he/161441.html (accessed June 17, 2010).

7. J. Lee Grady, "Dirty Little Secrets," Mastering Life Ministries, August 17, 2008, http://www.masteringlife.org/child-sexual-abuse/dirty-little-secrets (accessed June 17, 2010).

8. "Sexual Abuse Statistics," citing information from the US Department of Justice, the US Department of Health and Human Services, the Child Welfare League of America, the National Center on Child Abuse Prevention Research, and other organizations. Go to http://www.prevent-abuse-now.com/stats.htm. Government and private studies found that one-third of juvenile delinquents, 40 percent of sexual offenders, and 76 percent of serial rapists report they were sexually abused as youngsters.

9. "André Malraux Quotes," ThinkExist.com, http://thinkexist.com/quotation/what_is_man-a_miserable_little_pile_of/180697.html (accessed June 21, 2010).

10. Samuel Taylor Coleridge, "The Rime of the Ancient Mariner," *Lyrical Ballads* (n.p.: n.p., 1798), http://www.poemhunter.com/poem/rime-of-the-ancient-mariner-the/ (accessed June 17, 2010).

11. Charles Dickens, *A Christmas Carol* (London: Elliot Stock, 62, Paternoster Row, E.C., 1890), http://www.stormfax.com/1dickens.htm (accessed June 17, 2010).

12. Ibid.

13. *Fatal Attraction*, dir. Adrian Lyne (1987; n.p.: Paramount Home Video, 2002), DVD.

14. David Kyle Foster, *Sexual Healing* (n.p.: Regal Books, 2005).

15. Jerry Sutton, *A Simple Guide to the Way Back Home* (n.p.: Broadman and Holman Publishers, 2002).

16. Jim Bakker, *I Was Wrong* (Nashville, TN: Thomas Nelson, 1997).

17. J. Lee Grady, "What I Learned Behind Bars," *Charisma*, February 1997, 46–47.

18. Ibid.

LIE #9
REAL MEN DON'T CRY.

1. "Max Beckmann Quotes," BrainQuote.com, http://www.brainyquote.com/quotes/quotes/m/maxbeckman307427.html (accessed June 17, 2010).

2. "Jean Rhys Quotes," http://thinkexist.com/quotation/i_often_want_to_cry-that_is_the_only_advantage/210348.html (accessed June 17, 2010).

3. "Kurt Vonnegut Jr. Quotes," ThinkExist.com, http://thinkexist.com/quotation/laughter_and_tears_are_both_responses_to/13988.html (accessed June 17, 2010).

4. Rita Schiano, *Sweet Bitter Love* (n.p.: The Reed Edwards Company, 1997), as quoted at "Quotations About Crying," QuoteGarden.com, http://www.quotegarden.com/crying.html (accessed June 17, 2010).

5. "Christian Nevell Quotes," ThinkExist.com, http://thinkexist.com/quotes/christian_nevell_bovee/ (accessed June 17, 2010).

6. "Jewish Proverb Quotes," ThinkExist.com, http://thinkexist.com/quotation/what_soap_is_for_the_body-tears_are_for_the_soul/335741.html (accessed June 17, 2010).

7. "Billy Graham Quotes," ThinkExist.com, http://thinkexist.com/quotation/tears_shed_for_self_are_tears_of_weakness-but/326922.html (accessed June 17, 2010).

8. *Father of the Bride*, dir. Charles Shyer (1991; n.p: Touchstone Home Video, n.d.), DVD.

9. Watchman Nee, *Release of the Spirit* (n.p.: New Wine Press, 2007).

10. Ibid., 20–21.

11. George Whitefield quoted in Charles Spurgeon, *Lectures to My Students* (Grand Rapids, MI: Zondervan, 1954), 307.

12. Ibid.

13. Spurgeon, *Lectures to My Students*, 305.

14. Ibid., 309.

LIE #10

A MAN SHOULD NEVER RECEIVE SPIRITUAL MINISTRY FROM A WOMAN.

1. Tertullian, "*De Cultu Feminarum*," book 1, chapter 1, *Modesty in Apparel Becoming to Women in Memory of the Introduction of Sin Through a Woman,* in "The Ante-Nicene Fathers," http://www.tertullian.org/anf/anf04/anf04-06.htm (accessed June 18, 2010).

2. Origen, *Fragments on First Corinthians*, as quoted in Ruth A. Tucker and Walter L. Liefield, *Daughters of the Church* (Grand Rapids, MI: Zondervan, 1987), 106.

3. V. Bush, "Women Preachers," The Church of the Lord Jesus Christ of the Apostolic Faith, http://thechurch-apostolicfaith.org/womenpreachers.htm (asccessed June 18, 2010).

4. Aymon de Albatrus, "Kingdom of God vs. Women Preachers," Albatrus .org, http://www.albatrus.org/english/living/kingdom/kingdom_vs_women_ preachers.htm (accessed June 18, 2010).

5. Maureen Eha, "She Will Not Remain Silent," CharismaMag.com, May 13, 2002, http://www.charismamag.com/index.php/covers/260-cover -story/5988-she-will-not-remain-silent (accessed June 18, 2010).

6. Richard and Catherine Kroeger, *Women Elders: Called by God?* (Louisville, KY: Women's Ministry Unit, Presbyterian Church, U.S.A., 1980), 16.

7. John Chrysostom, *Commentary on Romans, Nicene and Postnicene Fathers*, first series, XL, 55, quoted in Kroeger, *Women Elders: Called by God?*, 17.

8. Richard and Catherine Kroeger, *I Suffer Not a Woman* (Grand Rapids, MI: Baker Book House, 1992), 87–98.

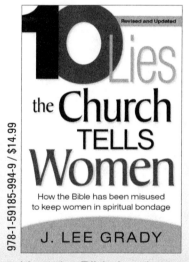
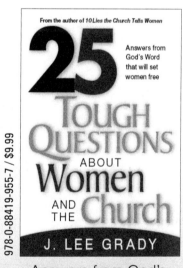

FREE NEWSLETTERS
TO HELP EMPOWER YOUR LIFE

Why subscribe today?

❑ **DELIVERED DIRECTLY TO YOU.** All you have to do is open your inbox and read.

❑ **EXCLUSIVE CONTENT.** We cover the news overlooked by the mainstream press.

❑ **STAY CURRENT.** Find the latest court rulings, revivals, and cultural trends.

❑ **UPDATE OTHERS.** Easy to forward to friends and family with the click of your mouse.

CHOOSE THE E-NEWSLETTER THAT INTERESTS YOU MOST:

- Christian news
- Daily devotionals
- Spiritual empowerment
- And much, much more

SIGN UP AT: **http://freenewsletters.charismamag.com**

8178